306.736 Dol
Dolesh, Daniel J.
Love me, love me not

WITHDRAWN

ON LINE

WITHDRAWN

D0105686

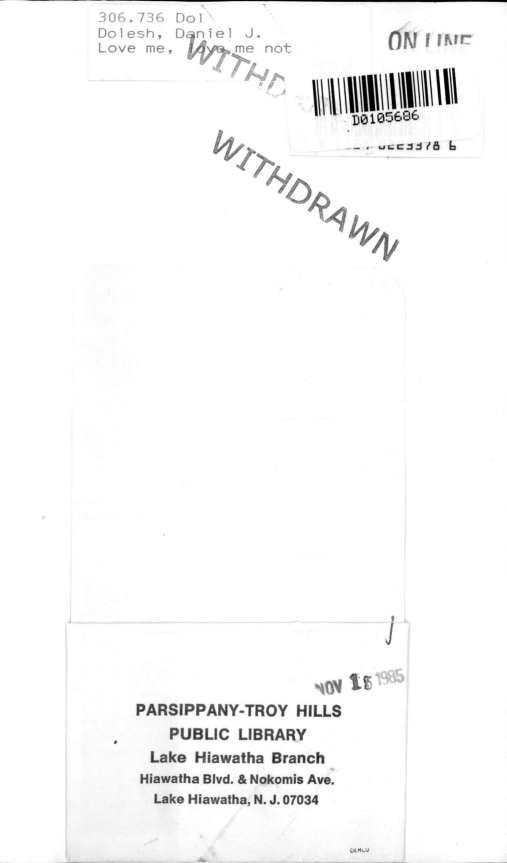

NOV 15 1985

PARSIPPANY-TROY HILLS
PUBLIC LIBRARY
Lake Hiawatha Branch
Hiawatha Blvd. & Nokomis Ave.
Lake Hiawatha, N. J. 07034

DEMCO

Love Me
Love Me Not

Love Me
Love Me Not

How to Survive Infidelity

Daniel J. Dolesh
and Sherelynn Lehman

McGraw-Hill Book Company

New York   St. Louis   San Francisco
Toronto   Hamburg   Mexico

Copyright © 1985 by Daniel J. Dolesh and Sherelynn Lehman
All rights reserved. Printed in the United States of America. Except as permitted under the Copyright
Act of 1976, no part of this publication may be reproduced or distributed in any form or by any means
or stored in a data base or retrieval system, without the prior written permission of the publisher.

1 2 3 4 5 6 7 8 9 D O C D O C 8 7 6 5

ISBN 0-07-017394-X

LIBRARY OF CONGRESS CATALOGING IN PUBLICATION DATA

Dolesh, Daniel J.
  Love me, love me not.
  1. Adultery.   2. Impediments to marriage.
I. Lehman, Sherelynn.   II. Title.
HQ806.D65   1985   306.7'36   85-7840
ISBN 0-07-017394-X

BOOK DESIGN BY PATRICE FODERO

To Dan, my partner
S.L.

To Sherry, my partner
D.D.

Contents

Acknowledgments

Most of all we would like to thank our children, who sat and waited so we could write:

Jennifer Lynn

Jonathan Daniel

Melanie Ann

Joshua Michael

Christopher Freeman

Michael Aaron

Jonathan Paul

and our housekeepers, who worked so we could write: Mary Robinson and Ethel Cunningham; and our editor, who made our unreadable readable: Lisa Frost.

Others contributed their skills and wisdom to this book in various ways: Dorothy Valerian, Shelly Bloomfield, Alice Rickel, Ed and Anna Dolesh and Marvin and Esther Friedman, and especially Sherri Foxman, who led and encouraged us. We thank all of them most sincerely.

Our gratitude also goes to the many we interviewed, especially "the group" of betrayed who sat through hours of questions and discussions about their experiences. They must remain anonymous, but their experiences and advice have inspired every page.

Introduction

Francine staggered into our office looking terrible. Her brown hair was disheveled, her eyes glazed, and her clothes rumpled.

"I need help," she moaned.

Her story was simple. Alan, her husband, a pillar of the community, had volunteered to teach Sunday school at their church. He team-taught with someone pretty and vivacious—more vivacious than Francine, or so it seemed. Francine saw signs of an affair but did not believe that *her* husband could be unfaithful. She heard whispers, but, as she told us, "I just thought it was the usual malicious gossip. Alan stayed later and later at the office, he and Diana had to prepare classes together, people talked." She believed none of it—until she found prophylactics in Alan's pocket. Francine had had a hysterectomy, so clearly the prophylactics were to be used with someone else.

She denied the affair's reality at first, but then confronted him. "Yes, I love her, but I still love you," he insisted. In shock she wept, screamed, and pleaded with him. For a while they pulled closer together. Their sex life became wildly creative. Still, Francine could not forget Alan's affair, though she did not understand the stages of devastation through which her emotions were passing.

Slowly her anger built into a consuming rage, and her marriage crumbled. She avoided friends and acquaintances, until those relationships, too, disintegrated. She performed more and more poorly at work —arriving late, arguing with colleagues, working in a fog of distraction— until her exasperated supervisor fired her.

After Alan left, Francine drifted for two years. She moved from one unsatisfying relationship to another, and ended each with the same sense of emptiness and failure. Her moods shifted wildly, like waves whipped up by a storm.

"Finally I became so bitter about people that I just said, 'The hell with everyone,' and became a loner. But it wasn't me," she explained— "I had always been outgoing and friendly. Alan didn't just leave me, he kicked me in the teeth. I felt rejected and betrayed. I just didn't give a damn about anyone or anything." One lonely Sunday afternoon, while soaking in a warm bath, she slit both her wrists.

Fortunately, the cuts were not deep enough, and an old friend who happened to stop by called for help. Eventually Francine came to us for counseling and began to pick up the pieces of a shattered life.

There were many preventative steps Francine could have taken before the affair ever took place, but she hadn't wanted to acknowledge the danger signs, hoping it was all a bad dream. Once she discovered the betrayal, had she understood her feelings and behavior, she could have learned a way to cope and taken some steps to prevent her downhill slide.

The final solution Francine attempted may have been drastic, but millions of people pass along a similar path. According to recent research, almost half of all marriages will have a third person enter the marital picture as the lover of either the husband or the wife. The pain and devastation for millions of spouses cannot be calculated. Sexual betrayal—betrayal by the one with whom you share your bed and your most intimate secrets—is one of the most devastating and destructive experiences a person can have. Its victims suffer shock, bitterness, frustration, and despair. Most do not know where to turn for help and so receive none.

As marriage and sex therapists we see a steady stream of betrayed people, such as Francine, come through our office door. We have searched through psychological literature for help in understanding what takes place in the psyche of a betrayed person and how he or she can best be aided. But although we found quite a bit written about people who have affairs, there was little about the person left behind. For the most part, the betrayed one was left to his or her own devices, which are practically nil in the face of such shock. Consequently, we began our own study of infidelity, hoping to shed some light for the many who might otherwise have to struggle with this experience in the dark. We wanted to give betrayed people a therapeutic resource that would explain their feelings, that would ease their pain, that would help them to respond—somewhere to turn for practical advice.

We began to research the dynamics of infidelity and studied hundreds of situations, interviewing nearly 500 people. As we analyzed the patterns of devastation and recovery, we determined that most individuals have the same basic emotional stages when trying to cope with infidelity. In some individuals the stages blend; in others, certain emotions recur. The amount of time spent in a particular stage can vary greatly from case to case. For the vast majority of people, however, the overall pattern is the same.

We have found that the stages we identified are applicable not only to those who are betrayed sexually but also to a variety of nonsexual betrayal situations. Some examples of situations closely related to sexual betrayal are an unexpected request for divorce (especially when the person asking for the divorce affirms that he or she no longer loves the other person), and sudden abandonment by a mate.

What is the practical value of identifying stages of emotional reaction to betrayal, other than providing insight into one's situation and life process? If these stages can be identified, then a structure for therapeutic growth can be created. By knowing what to expect, one is able to prepare for and cushion the impact of what is to come.

Love Me, Love Me Not is divided into two sections. In the first, we explore the signs and causes of infidelity and describe the five stages of emotional reaction to the discovery of an affair. We help the betrayed one to understand his or her feelings and to cope with them, thereby assisting the healing process. In the second section, we guide the betrayed in choosing whether to rebuild the damaged relationship or to let go and take a different direction. We also offer practical advice on using legal aid and community and religious resources, on dealing with children, and on rebuilding a relationship or returning to the single life.

To illustrate the stages of reaction through which "the one left behind" almost invariably passes, we offer the experiences of seven individuals representative of the hundreds of cases we studied. Not all of
the seven joined the group at the same stage: some had just discovered
the betrayal in their lives, others had already moved through the stages
of reaction and were making decisions for the future. Each handled
betrayal in his or her own way—their responses and strategies differed,
and their various relationships went down different paths—but all seven
went through the same stages of reaction. And, apart from some of the
details of their particular situations (which have been changed to pre-
serve their anonymity), their stories are universal.

   Marilyn is 52 years old. Her dark hair is cut short—"sporty"—and
is graying in front. Quiet and pleasant, Marilyn does not draw attention
to herself with clothes and makeup. As the oldest member of the group,
she is cast by the others as a kind of matriarch—a role in which she
is uncomfortable, given her basically shy nature. They tend to look to
her for wisdom and sobriety, even though her own feelings and experiences were dramatic in the extreme. Marilyn is sophisticated, and it
is easy to imagine her in the tennis clubs and charitable civic organizations to which she once belonged. But her world has drastically changed.
Six months ago she divorced her husband, Carl. Now, unemployed and
on her own, she feels lost. Alimony will help, but her loss was more
than that of money. Her focus in life was to be Carl's helpmate, first
while he finished medical school and then as he established a practice.
Carl needed her, her friends needed her, and her organizations needed
her. Now Carl is gone, and no one relies on Marilyn.
   Gerald, at 34, is a full professor, seen on campus as an intellectual
lion: tenured, published, and successful. His personality, reflecting his
mind, is precise and logical. One wonders how Gerald could have
married Marina, unless it is true that opposites attract. An actress, she
dresses in jeans and a sweatshirt, no bra, long earrings, and sandals.
She moves with artists and poets, while Gerald spends most of his time
with other professors whom Marina scorns as ivory-towered intellectuals.
They have no children but never really intended to have children. They
always considered themselves liberals: Gerald an intellectual liberal
and Marina a cultural liberal. Then came Marina's affair, and Gerald's
open-mindedness ran into a dead-end. It all seemed totally illogical to

him. "I was a good husband and a good lover. What more could she possibly want?"

Francine, 31, of whom we've already spoken, is pretty and extroverted. She is keenly perceptive, with an engaging wit; as she speaks, a smile flits on and off her lips. In the group she is a natural leader and tends to defend her own judgments strongly. Once she's made up her mind about something, it is almost impossible to convince her otherwise. For instance, she was convinced that her husband was *not* having an affair, even though all the signs indicated he was. "How could someone so religious and active in church have an affair?" she shouted at the group one night in impotent frustration. "He was practically a man of the cloth!" Francine always prided herself on her ability to see both sides of an issue—until she was stunned by the realization that her conservative husband was having an affair with a religion teacher. Francine and her husband have been separated for two years but are not yet divorcing.

Craig, like Francine, is outgoing and strong-minded. Outwardly, he is rough and tumble, able to "roll with the punches"—or so he thought. Starting at the bottom of life's ladder, he worked his way through school while his father drank. He began as a waiter, cleverly worked his way up to being manager, and eventually bought the restaurant. Recently he has franchised, and besides restaurants he owns apartments and other real estate. He takes time off now, because at 44 he has enough money to last the rest of his life. A fascinating conversationalist, he injected much humor into the group and often suggested solutions for others' problems, but it took quite a few sessions before he told his own story. He advised others to "live it up, try new things, new ideas!" "Look at me," he quipped. "All work and no play made Craig a dull boy. I spent most of my time making money and then could not understand how my wife could have been so ungrateful as to go to bed with someone else." That someone else turned out to be his best friend and tennis partner.

Angela, at 28, is the youngest of the group. Her long blond hair and tinted glasses give her a Gloria Steinem look. Very intellectual, she enrolled in a doctoral program at Georgetown University after working for several years in public relations. She speaks her mind and is deeply committed to her values. The words "right and wrong" pop up in her conversation, and she is dedicated to causes such as the environment and antinuclear issues. Angela felt that she could handle just about anything, even an affair if Rick wanted to have one. "But why would he?" she asked. "Our sex life was dynamite. We did just about everything there was to do and then some. Still, I probably could have handled an ordinary betrayal." Maybe she could have, but her lover's betrayal was not "ordinary," at least not in her mind.

Phil, who is 25 and runs a small electrical business, is still living with his wife. As far as everyone can see, they are the perfect couple. Phil believes in family, always attending family reunions and solicitous of his parents. He is a traditionalist at heart, although he would never describe himself that way. His business relies on local trade, and he is active in the community, attending Rotary Club meetings and singing in the church choir. He feels a strong sense of loyalty to his wife, Ellen. To the community they appear the ideal young couple: he a hard-working and successful businessman and she the dutiful wife, keeping the books and taking care of their children. Ellen is dedicated and loving—except when she is in bed with one of Phil's employees.

Joan is 39 years old and a self-assured businesswoman, the vice president of a local bank in charge of the loan department. She has always driven herself hard, setting her goals and then attaining them. "I may not have as much time for my family as other women," she argues, "but, damn it, I provide well for them, very well indeed." Like Phil, she has not separated from her husband of six years, Hal, and they share the responsibility of raising their two preschool children. Joan radiates self-control and organization. Her short-cropped blond hair is meticulously brushed. She always smiles, but an air of sadness seems to hang about her, giving the impression that she smiles because she is supposed to smile. Her self-composure is fraying at the edges; her world, which she has so ably held together for the last six years, is finally coming apart.

With these seven people we will take a journey. The journey begins with the shock of discovery, moves along a rocky road of emotional upheaval, and leads to self-knowledge and renewal.

1

Seeing the Signs
of Betrayal

Cracks etch their way up the eggshell of a relationship before it breaks. Jagged, unmistakable lines, there for all to see. A person having an affair leaves signs along the road, and if one cares or dares to read carefully, the direction of those signs becomes clear.

Sometimes the person leaving the clues wants and demands attention in this way. It is a plaintive cry of desperation from the betrayer. "Look at me," he or she says, "don't you see what is happening? I have no other way of communicating with you. My lovemaking with someone else will force you to take notice. You *will* pay attention to me!"

In other instances the betrayer wants the affair to be kept a secret. It may have started as a lark, an exciting game to break the daily routine. Possibly it was an attempt to defy the rules, or maybe it started during a weak moment—at a convention or after too much alcohol. In any case, the betrayer did not want the affair to become known. Even with the intention of keeping the affair secret, however, traces are almost always left behind. Still, the person betrayed often cannot see what is happening, refusing to interpret the signs and face reality. "It was so obvious," bemoaned Francine "—after it happened. It seemed everyone had known about it beforehand except me. How could I have been so stupid?"

"Not stupid," corrected Joan, "just blind. I think we all become blind when something like this happens. We twist our insides around to keep from facing the conclusion. I knew it, deep down I knew it, but I just could not bring myself to accept what was going on. All the little signs were there. He'd come home late from work. He started to travel more and would go out of town for weekends. Our acquaintances began to act strangely when they were around us—almost as if they were taking sides.

"I remember Hal going on a diet. He started to jog and I knew he hated to jog. He was happy as a clam most of the time. Wore cologne, the bastard. He would never wear it when we would go out. But still I did not put two and two together."

Most of the betrayed people we interviewed agreed that they were the last ones to realize that their mates were having an affair, even though the evidence was all around them. There were many trivial activities that in retrospect indicated that something was amiss. Above all there was a change in their relationship with their mates. A movement away from intimacy began—a mutual reluctance to get too close. Their relationships with their spouses may already have been in difficult straits, but now there was a subtle refusal to mend the tattered edges. Sexual patterns changed, and many times the married couple stopped having sex altogether.

Some who have affairs move away from their partners angrily and with confrontation, while others attempt to escape intimacy quietly and with as little pain as possible.

The angry ones try to exonerate themselves and alleviate their feelings of guilt by blaming the situation, the raw deal life has given them, pressures at work, children, and especially mates who, they feel, don't understand what they really need.

"My God," said Craig one evening during a discussion period, "she kept trying to blame me for everything going wrong in our marriage. It was like she was trying to punish me for what she was doing, even though I didn't know at the time that she was having an affair. I remember one night she came home late and started to blame me for not going to the bank that day. 'I forgot,' I told her, 'I just plain forgot. It's no big deal.' Then she really hit the ceiling. 'Nothing's a big deal to you,' she screamed. 'You always have everything under control, don't you? Mr.

Perfect.' Now I look back on what happened and I can see what she meant. She was angry because I wasn't out of control; she was the one who was out of control and she was trying to blame me. The whole thing was back-asswards."

Angry betrayers try to blame their spouses for the deterioration of their relationships. If the betrayers can convince themselves that it is their spouses' fault, then they feel somewhat more justified in having the affair. In this sorry way they attain a type of permission for having the affair and thereby alleviate some of their guilt. In order to accomplish this, however, they cannot allow their spouses to come too close, lest the façade of blame they are building crumble and the "permission" or justification for their affair be snatched away.

The betrayer who does not express anger needs to move away from his or her partner just like the angry blamer, but this betrayer attempts to back out quietly and without accusatorial flair. The effect is the same, however: the betrayer avoids intimacy with his or her spouse, and pushing him or her away seems to justify the affair. "See, we weren't getting along. It was really a bad marriage." We can call this second type of person the anxious avoider.

The partner of the anxious avoider may realize that the relationship is crumbling and make a move to revitalize it, but the betrayer is moving in the opposite direction. Attempts to increase affection or intimacy only increase the guilt the anxious avoider is already experiencing. The mannerisms and habits of his or her spouse become tedious and eventually irksome. The person having an affair may develop what psychologists call a sexual aversion: the very sight of his or her spouse naked becomes disgusting, and he or she may cringe from the touch of the other.

Phil told the group: "We used to have good sex and enjoyed one another at one time. Then Ellen began to act as though she didn't even want to touch me. I remember lying in bed and reaching over to touch her breast. She would actually jerk away a little; she couldn't seem to control it. I don't know what was so unappetizing about me. At one time she used to enjoy my body. I'm a little bit older than when we first met, but I don't think that I've changed that much. I tried to talk about it with her, but she clammed up and backed away. I felt lost. What can you do when your wife won't even talk about how she feels? I kept asking her what I was doing wrong—somehow I thought it was my fault, that I was doing something she didn't like, that I had lost my touch sexually. I should have known then that she was sleeping with someone else."

Anxious avoiders cannot bear to increase their feelings of guilt. They cannot confront their spouses, they cannot tell them about the affair. They are panic-stricken by the thought of asking for a divorce. This is the type of person who after twenty-five years of marriage might leave a note telling his or her spouse that it's all over and that he or she is running away with someone else. One abandoned wife showed us a note she found on the kitchen counter one bleak morning when she went down to make coffee for breakfast:

Dear ———
    I am so sorry and ashamed. I do not know how to tell you this, so I figured a letter was better. We have not been getting along together for a long time now. You don't really seem to care for me any more. I feel terrible that I have to leave you, but I think it is better for both of us. I have grown quite close to ———. I feel it is better if I go with her. I took some things I needed from the house last night. I will come back later for more things after the shock of this wears off for you.
    I still care a whole lot for you and the children and I think you are a wonderful person.

                                        Affectionately,
                                        ———

This note was left after twenty-eight years of marriage! Not a spoken word of good-bye after three children and all those years of investment. What a pity that this woman could not read the signs and take action before this happened.

Knowing the Signs

Look around you and read the signs, but beware of being overly suspicious. Every little sign may not point to infidelity. Don't become paranoid and jump at each one. Some have called unwarranted suspicion about the sexual activity of one's mate or lover the "Othello syndrome," after the Shakespearean character whose distrust and jealousy led him to destroy the woman he loved so passionately. If you constantly look for signs of betrayal, even after it has been proved that no such betrayal has occurred, you might just fulfill your own prophecy. We know one businessman who could not stand for his wife to speak with other men. He worried when she was alone at home during the day, convinced as he was that she was looking for an affair with every mailman and meter reader who came by the house. Eventually, his wife became so distraught over his jealousy and accusations that she stormed out, slamming the door behind her. "See," he wailed miserably, "I knew it all the time. That's why she's leaving me."

More often, however, people just refuse to perceive what is taking place all around them. Signs may be staring them in the face and they still cannot accept the fact that they are being betrayed. The following are some of the indications that an affair is taking place.

Silence

Silence creeps in like a heavy fog, enveloping your living space. You may not even know when it starts or from whence it comes. But it sits between you with an aching heaviness. Occasionally the silence may be broken by animated conversation, but soon you fall back to strained politeness. The silence may be a mask for anger, or it may be a sign of the unfaithful one's preoccupation: he or she wants to be with someone else.

Sexual Changes

Sexual changes can be of a positive or negative type. There may suddenly be a flurry of highly erotic lovemaking, but eventually, as the experience of those in the group indicated, an avoidance of sexual activity is established.

Many of those interviewed indicated that when a spouse begins an affair, sexual activity blossoms, often with new variations. This is because an affair can heighten the overall erotic mood of the betrayer. The betrayer may also be guiltily trying to please his or her spouse while struggling with an illicit affair. Several participants said they felt that their spouses were trying to tell them something.

Francine put it this way: "I could not understand why suddenly we were having sex all the time. And it was great sex! But it was a little too frantic—it was almost work. I once asked Alan why he was so amorous, but he really didn't answer me. After I found out about the affair I had this insight that he was really trying in his own way to tell me 'good-bye.' I hate him now for that deception. I actually thought our relationship was getting better!"

Eventually the increased sexual activity abates. There are fewer kisses hello and good-bye, and eventually there are no kisses at all. The betrayer hugs his or her side of the bed and jerks away when touched by his or her spouse. Men report that their unfaithful wives cried when they had intercourse. Craig said, "I tried to be more gentle, but nothing seemed to help. She just did not want to be touched. Afterwards she told me that it felt like she was being raped when we made love—or should I say, when we had sex?"

Working More

"I'll be working late again tonight, dear," has become a refrain—and this perhaps from someone who used to swear that only slaves worked more than they were paid for. Then there are the long lunches. Your spouse's secretary doesn't seem to know where he or she is when you phone the office. When you call later, your spouse explains that he or she was caught up with a client and can't even remember where they were.

The New Wardrobe

Your husband used to wear baggy pants and old shirts with frayed collars. Whenever you tried to get him to shop for clothes he would argue that he liked clothes that were "broken in"—meaning that he first wore them when he was in college, fifteen years ago. Suddenly, he comes home with a new suit; he has a new tie with a designer label and a pale pink shirt. "Need to upgrade my image at the office," he says. "Getting ready to ask for a promotion." You wonder how the new cologne he's wearing will help him get a promotion.

Or your wife comes home with the latest hairstyle and she's had her hair colored slightly, yet she's a woman who never even wore perfume because it was "too phony." *Au naturel* was her motto. And now she is wearing a new silk blouse, cut lower than she would ever dare before, designer jeans, and high heels—to a Weight Watchers meeting. You also happen to notice two new see-through nightgowns in the closet, and when she dressed this morning she put on a black bra and panties that had a little red rose on the side. When you question her about the nightgowns, she says, "Oh, those. I was saving them as a surprise. Thought I would wait until we went on a trip."

The New Body

Along with the new wardrobe may come a new body. Your spouse, whose primary exercise used to be lifting a fork to his or her mouth, is now out jogging at six in the morning (in a designer jogging suit, no less), getting on the scale every other day, and eating health food. All of this, plus the special-delivery exercise bike and the new health spa membership may well make you a little suspicious.

Marco Polo

A little travel was always part of your spouse's work, but now he or she seems to have become a correspondent for *National Geographic*. The excuses become more vague as he or she leaves for yet another weekend away: "I really don't know where I'll be staying, but I'll call and tell you—if I have a chance." You just can't understand how such a highly organized person can have meetings twenty-four hours a day and can't find the time to make a simple call. And some of the meeting locations might seem a little too exotic—like when he or she tells you, "I know a week in Honolulu sounds romantic to you, but it will be nothing but hard work for me. I'd like you to come along, but what would you do there without me around?"

Maybe your wife seems to have more and more activities and belong to clubs that take trips. "A group of us are going. I will probably be staying at someone's house," she explains. "You know how these groups try to save money." And now she goes grocery shopping every other day instead of weekly, and always in the late afternoon or evening. Two hours for a half-gallon of milk and a dozen eggs? And you already have two gallons of milk and three dozen eggs.

Mood Swings

A person having an affair lives on an emotional roller coaster. Your spouse starts the day full of energy and vitality, with eyes sparkling and a warm kiss good-bye for you, but that same day, as you are both getting ready for bed, explodes violently in anger. You feel like you are living with Dr. Jekyll and Mr. (or Mrs.) Hyde, and the tension is thick and heavy. Your spouse becomes angry for days at a time for no apparent reason; the littlest things become major issues. He or she demands changes of you, suddenly doesn't like the way you do this or that. At other times your spouse is pleasant and happy; he or she makes love to you and treats you with sweetness and consideration. You are given gifts—especially when he or she travels—and your anniversary and birthday are remembered. But you now know that this outpouring of affection and consideration is only temporary.

Withering Intimacy

The most important sign. Your spouse pulls away and refuses to share tender and meaningful moments with you. He or she denies to both of you the experience of intimacy. The feeling of closeness is eroding: you spend less and less time together, and your conversation is mostly superficial. Even though you are living with someone, you begin to feel lonely.

Of course, no one of these signs constitutes proof that your spouse is having an affair. But if you can state that most of these signs exist, your relationship is deteriorating—whether your spouse is having an affair or not—and your marriage will end unless you take steps to begin a healing process.

Facing Fear

Change induces fear. People become fearful when their world changes and they are not sure how to adjust. They become even more fearful if they do not know why their world is changing. They feel that they are losing control.

When a spouse begins to change, he or she becomes a stranger, someone frightening. Out of fear, then, many people let the signs pass and pretend that nothing is happening. To avoid the painful truth, they bury their heads in the sand like the proverbial ostrich. Like philosophical Cartesians, they believe that if they don't *think* it is happening then it really isn't happening. Would that it were so simple.

Gerald described how he avoided the pain of realization as long as he could. In his story we can see many of the signs he refused to read:

"My grandfather's death was like my wife's affair. He died about ten years ago. It was a long business, his dying. He had prostate cancer; it had spread to his lungs first, then his liver. For two years the doctors kept finding more cancer here and there, and Grandpa got sicker and sicker. There was a lot of ceremony around his dying. Children and grandchildren visited him in shifts, took turns with him over the holidays, helped him wrap up loose ends and loose memories. Toward the end we were all weary and empty. But do you want to know something? When it happened—when the hospital called us in just after dawn one morning—we were all shocked! I thought then that death is always a shock, even when it's sat right there with you for the longest time, long enough for you to get used to the idea.

"I thought about the shock of my grandfather's death when I found out about my wife's affair. I'd lived so long with the sense that she was sleeping with someone else, yet I was overturned when I found out for sure. I felt like I was a bowling pin the second the ball hits it—slam, up in the air, down with a crash, then swept away. Even though I'd known in my heart for months.

"About the time it started, I'd changed teaching jobs. The new job meant more money, more status, and a good opportunity. The only hitch was that the campus was about an hour and fifteen minutes away. Marina didn't want to move, even though it made sense. She was teaching a couple of acting courses at the local community center and was involved in a production, and she had a pretty tight circle of friends. So I commuted. What with early classes, office hours, committee meetings, and so forth, I found I was leaving early in the mornings and coming in late at night. Marina came in late, too, and it became later and later. Often she wouldn't get in from rehearsal until after midnight. I asked her why she was so late. She turned it back on me. 'You're the one who's gone all the time. What difference does it make if I'm late?' What could I say? She poked her fingers through her heavy black hair and, scrutinizing her face in the mirror, squeezed a blackhead with a detachment that always bothered me. She pulled further away from me in subtle ways. The quick kiss good-bye wasn't there. She didn't hook her arm in mine the way she used to when we would walk down the street. Many little things. But I thought this was just her. She always was hard.

"I believe in delicate sensibilities—not the kind that come out of dry custom, you understand, but the kind that come out of a sense of ourselves as special. Marina was completely insensitive about herself.

She didn't need the flattery of special treatment or romance, or at least that's what I thought.

"I'd drive to work in the morning and meditate on my marriage. I wondered what was wrong between us long before I knew for certain that *he* existed. I knew that something had flattened in our relationship. I even speculated in the abstract about her having an affair. But for some reason I could never perceive the signs that she really *was* unfaithful.

"Then I saw her begin to change. As hard as she was, she seemed to soften. She let her hair grow longer, 'more feminine' as she said one day. She had rarely worn perfume; now she carried it in her purse. The old jeans and T-shirt were gone. She even started wearing skirts.

"Sometimes it was sitting there in front of me, like Grandpa's death. When Marina wasn't around, our friends would ask me with slight innuendo, 'How are you two getting along?' 'Fine. Just fine,' I'd reply. I could never bring myself to follow their gentle lead and say, 'Why do you ask?'

" 'A few of us went out for drinks after rehearsal,' she said one night. 'Oh, who?' 'Rob and, let's see, Carly, Stan, and Whizzer.' Another time, 'Some of us think that when the show's finished here we should take it over to the army base.' 'Who thinks so?' 'Rob, of course, Donna, and Ty.'

"Rob 'of course' McIlhenny was going to be making love to my wife. I couldn't think of it as an accomplished fact at the time, but down deep it was in front of me, sitting with me for the longest time. The next time I saw him I shook his hand with gusto, both of us sensing the unspoken mystery between us.

"So my wife had a special male friend. Many women have platonic relationships, I told myself. Somewhere inside I wanted to see Marina lose control over something. I wanted to find out what could make her jumpy, devious, steamy. Rob put his arm around her, and I was filled with doubt. She seemed as impervious to him as she was to me. Maybe I was wrong. Maybe I was wrong! The feeling was one of intense relief.

"In my game with myself, I was gambling my intuition against my belief in the utter consistency of Marina's character. To her, dreams, romance, crushing embraces were 'twaddle.' If I had misunderstood her, after an eight-year 'workshop' in her, then who *was* she? I believed in her like I believed in God. Besides, marriages just don't end—at least

I couldn't imagine mine ending. My parents never got divorced, nor did my grandparents.

"On the night of the last performance, Marina sat at the dressing table, cold-creaming the makeup off her face. The rest of the cast had already gone to the party at Stan's house. 'We'll be along soon,' she said, waving everyone out. 'I need to wind down,' she told me. 'Sit and watch me get this goop off my face.'

" 'What a treat,' I said.

" 'Then go along with the others. I can get a ride with Rob.'

" 'Of course. He'll be *so* happy.'

" 'Huh?' Her face was a blot of white cream, her two dark eyes burning exceptions.

" 'Never mind.' Suddenly I felt giddy. First and last time. I don't know where the words came from, but I said it. 'You know,' I said, 'for a while there it looked like you were sleeping with Rob.'

"She stopped wiping, her tissue poised, and we looked at each other in the mirror. 'For a while there,' she said, starting to wipe again, 'I was.'

"Strike. Up in the air. Down with a crash. Swept away.

"Why didn't I see? I had thought she wouldn't sleep with someone else because I couldn't imagine dreams of romance trespassing across her mind. And dreams of romance, I thought, were the stuff of affairs. So I thought and rationalized. Dreams of romance, I suddenly saw, are only what affairs seem to be about to other people.

"Something surged up in me. I was drowning with fury. In probably the only savage act of my entire life, I hurled myself at her, knocked her onto the floor, and we struggled for a while in some vague, stupid way. Then the pushing and tearing turned into gestures of a different kind. It wasn't lovemaking. There wasn't any love to be made, but she was still mine. It was hard and ugly—and better than it had been in years. So much for romance."

Gerald had had all the indications—indications from Marina, from others, from inside himself—but he refused to recognize the very signs that were tormenting him. He tried to maintain control by not accepting the reality of what was taking place. When Marina finally told him and he could no longer deny it, he made a last desperate, physical attempt to regain control.

Fear of finding out can motivate you to do everything in your power not to look. You don't want to know that you have been betrayed by the one you love. You don't want to consider that your relationship with someone who has played such an important part in your life might be cracking apart. There is something basic and primitive in us all that compels us to trust the person to whom we are sexually committed. When that trust is twisted and snapped we feel a great pain. The sensation is akin to the pain we feel when we have lost someone dear through death. It is a pain we try to avoid at all costs.

If you see a crack in your relationship and feel the threat of imminent danger, be aware of this natural avoidance tendency and do your best to resist it. You must face your fear and the unknown if you are to take hold of your life and make changes for the future.

You must recognize the fear that is slowly twisting your insides in painful tension. This is not easy, because we often displace the anxiety of a threat to our personality or the fear of a specific danger onto other persons or onto bodily functions. You may find that you are having trouble sleeping—possibly waking up early in the morning before your usual rising time. Your eyelids may twitch in an annoying way or your legs cramp when you are in bed. You may find that you have become more irritable or that you stay up late at night working crossword puzzles, playing video games, or doing some other repetitive activity. Once you face the fear and say, "Yes, I'm afraid," you can move on to identify its source. Once you get to the root of your fear and shine a spotlight on it, you'll find dangers are no longer so ominous as they seemed when they lurked in the shadows.

You will have to search within yourself, either through quiet reflection or through conversation with a counselor or a friend, for the source of your fears. You might consider the following possibilities:

- My spouse doesn't love me anymore.
- My spouse is going to abandon me and I'll be all alone.
- I am worthless.
- I am going to lose control.
- I don't know what to do.
- All my friends will lose respect for me.

Having determined the danger, you can now defuse it. There are several methods you can use to do this.

Imagine the worst.   After you identify your fear, imagine the worst possible scenario. For someone this might be, "She will come home, tell me she no longer loves me, and abandon me and the children." As unpleasant as this scenario may be, you can still draw some positive conclusions. For instance, "The situation is not impossible: I can hire a housekeeper, I may meet someone else, and I'll be free from the tension of the past." Gradually you can ease your panic as you consider that even the worst possible situation would be manageable.

Take one small step at a time.   Even though you will have to take action, you need not do everything at once. To cope with your fears and the dangers of acknowledging the possibility of your spouse's infidelity, you must develop a plan of action which will permit you to either heal your relationship with your spouse or to end the marriage and strike out on your own. But your plan should focus on one step at a time. A feasible plan will give you security and more control over the situation.

Be realistic.   Don't expect that the sense of danger you feel as you read the clues pointing toward a possible affair will evaporate. The danger, if not of an affair, then at least of a deteriorating marriage, may be, and probably is, very real. Still, as Sigmund Freud discovered, anxiety does have a function; it is a signal that your ego emits, warning of some conflict. Fear, then, can be an ally, a healthy reaction to danger. It prods you to be alert, to marshal your resources, and to prepare for the future. If you find the signs of betrayal in your relationship, you do have something to fear. Hiding from the danger and acting in panic is unrealistic and destructive. Facing your fear and using it to meet the challenge is your best and only hope for future happiness.

2

What to Do If You Suspect

It's important to remember that at this point you don't know for sure whether your spouse is emotionally and sexually involved with someone else. Right now you might have only some nagging doubts. Someone may have made a passing comment. Maybe you've begun to worry about some changes in your spouse's personality. Or possibly you noticed the change in bed.

Francine told us in one of our discussions that for her it was like seeing the pieces of a puzzle come together in slow motion: "It all seemed to point in one direction. In the pit of my stomach I got a sinking feeling. Something was wrong, dreadfully wrong. I looked a little further and it all started to add up. 'My God,' I muttered to myself one evening when I was making supper for the kids and me and Alan was late again. 'It could be true.' Something surged up in me—fear, panic, I'm not sure what. I could feel my stomach muscles tighten, and I began to cry softly. Mikey came up and asked me what was wrong. 'Did you get hurt?' he asked."

The clues may be many, and may all seem to add up to one conclusion, but it's hard to be sure. You never really can be sure until you have evidence in black and white or until someone you believe tells you that such is the case. "What do I do?" you might wonder. "Do I confront my spouse, demand that the affair be broken off? Should I see a lawyer first, protect myself?" The idea of your spouse being in love with someone else turns your anxiety to panic.

What should you do if you are faced with the probability that your lover or spouse is having an affair? First, sit down and try to calm yourself. Of course, it's not easy to be calm when you feel that your world is exploding around you. Your system is pumping adrenaline. You want to jump up and run, fight, *do* something. But we must emphasize that at this critical time you must sit down, calm yourself, and think. Consider your options *before* you act. If you act before you've carefully formulated a strategy, you could do immeasurable harm to yourself and to your relationship.

One option is to "wait and see." "That's what I did," said Joan. "I waited. I think I was secretly hoping that it would all go away and that I would not have to deal with it. Boy, was that a mistake. I might have been able to do something about it, but I blew it by doing nothing." Joan did "blow it," as she said. Her husband *was* having an affair, and her relationship with him got worse and worse. She knew that she had to do something, but she remained paralyzed, as if caught in a spider web that wound about her tighter and tighter, choking off her doubts and clouding her perceptions.

To "wait and see" is useless. Nothing is accomplished, and valuable time is lost. Joan's relationship was deteriorating, and she could have made some moves either to salvage the marriage or to terminate it. Either would have eased her shock and pain, and she could have acted from a position of strength. Not to act is suicide.

A second option is to confront your spouse, to demand to know what is going on and why. This is the response recommended by most authors. "Confront your spouse and ask him or her if he or she is having an affair. Demand to know if the answer is evasive," says one author. We strongly disagree with this approach. First, it can be disastrous to jump to the conclusion that you are being betrayed sexually unless you have indisputable evidence. It can not only send you into an emotional tailspin, but could, if you act on an erroneous assumption, irreparably damage your marriage. Accusing a truly committed spouse could greatly upset that person and attack the trust you might share. If your mate *is* having an affair, your confrontation will be taken as a frontal attack, and his or her defenses will quickly shoot up. Angry denials will follow, and you will both feel hurt and distrustful. Nothing constructive will be accomplished.

Will your suspicion be erased if you confront the other person and he or she denies that an affair is taking place? Probably not, because any confrontation is apt to provoke a denial. Will a confrontation stop gossip which may be occurring? Again, probably not, unless your spouse stops the affair. But he or she will not stop the affair unless you take other action to improve your relationship.

A third option is to broadcast your misgivings. This was Phil's approach. "I felt this need to tell everyone about my suspicion. It was such a burden. Maybe I thought that if I told other people the load wouldn't be so heavy on me."

Gerald disagreed with his explanation. "Maybe you were just trying to win other people over to your side," he argued.

"I think you were trying to wreck her reputation," chimed in Craig. "That way you didn't have to blame yourself if it was true."

"Well, you may both be right," replied Phil, "because I told everybody. I probably even told the mailman. I did wonder at the time whether I was just trying to win everyone over to my side in order to prove that she was a rat."

Any of the reasons the group discussed may have been true. In any case, to tell friends or relatives about your suspicions could be even more harmful than the other options. You are harming someone's reputation before you are sure of the facts, and you are broadcasting a great deal about your relationship. Your spouse is apt to hear it from someone else eventually and will become angry and less agreeable in rebuilding your relationship. Juicy gossip can spread very quickly, despite promises of "I'll never tell a soul" or "You can trust me." Friends and relatives are usually too close to the situation to give you unbiased advice. The natural tendency is to take sides. If your suspicions eventually prove to be untrue, or even if they are true, and you ride out the storm together, it will be very difficult to rebuild the relationships you have had with friends and relatives as a couple.

A fourth option, which many in the group confessed to using to some degree, is to snoop. The desire to snoop normally occurs after the discovery and denial stages, but may occur before a discovery. Some of the group members told us it was almost impossible not to pry. They spoke of a burning desire to discover, to find out for sure. Like moths circling a flame, they came closer and closer until they got burned. Some searched through purses or wallets, pockets, drawers, closets, briefcases, anywhere a clue might be found. Others looked carefully for an unfamiliar hair on a suit coat or sweater or for lipstick marks, or sniffed for the lingering smell of someone else's cologne. Some set traps. One said he was going out but instead sat in his car around the corner and watched the house. Angela described her attempt to find out by entrapment. "You remember Joanie, don't you? She said she saw you last night with someone cute and it wasn't me." One woman we interviewed related the following story:

"Jack told me he was going to be home late on Wednesday night because he was having an evening meeting with some clients from out of town. He said they were going to meet at the Hilton and he might just as well stay overnight because they could go very late. A likely story, I thought. A business meeting at night! And at the Hilton, no less! Who did he think he was kidding?

"I figured I would snoop and catch him. Half an hour before his meeting was to start, I positioned myself in an inconspicuous seat in the lobby and held a newspaper up in front of my face. I had just enough room to look around the edge of the paper.

"Sure enough, about five minutes before the meeting was to begin, he strolled through the lobby with his secretary. Young enough to be his daughter, and really cute. Aha, I thought, I'm right. I've got you now, you bastard.

"Well, feeling terribly cunning and clever, I already had a plan worked out. After they passed, I followed and watched which room they went into. Then I went into the hotel bar and had two vodkas on the rocks. My insides were churning. I waited about half an hour and went back to the room I had seen them enter earlier. I tiptoed to the door and knocked softly. When someone began to open the door I pushed it open as hard as I could, knocking over the person who opened it, and leapt into the room. 'Aha!' I yelled. There was my husband, frozen and stunned, sitting at a table with five other persons, notes and briefcases spread out around them. Fortunately, my husband kept his job, and the following month he began to speak to me again."

Snooping can be destructive to a relationship, but we realize that some people feel an almost irresistible urge to find out for sure. If you feel this way, we recommend that you first discuss the situation with an attorney and that, if at all possible, you hire someone professionally trained and experienced as an investigator to snoop for you. Your attorney can provide you with recommendations and cautions in this matter.

So these four options—the "wait-and-see," the "confrontation," the "broadcast," and the "snoop"—are usually more destructive than helpful. Does that mean that you must do nothing? Absolutely not! Now is the time to act, to take control of your life and your relationship, and move with firmness and resolution. Carefully evaluate your relationship and demand changes where they're needed. Keep in mind the following guidelines:

1. For help, turn to a professional. If you suspect that your spouse is unfaithful, you probably feel lost and alone, and you need support. You can't turn to your spouse, however, and we've already recommended above that you not broadcast your suspicions to your family and friends. But you do need to talk to someone. Marilyn told us: "When the suspicion begins to gnaw on you, you feel all alone. An icy chill creeps over you, and you don't know where to turn for someone to hold you and tell you it will be all right."

You need to air your suspicions. Sometimes, speaking the words and unburdening yourself can have a very liberating effect. First, it may help you place the whole situation in perspective and allow you to evaluate it more clearly; you will be less distraught and more rational when you have to make decisions and plan a course of action. Second, it may help you to feel that you can share your load with someone who is sympathetic, that there is a kind and confidential ear available. Third, it may help you to find that there are many persons in similar circumstances, that you are not alone in confronting this problem.

With whom should you speak? You can speak with a local priest, minister, or rabbi. Some of the clergy, especially those who have been trained as pastoral counselors, can be excellent listeners and provide good advice. However, you must realize that a religious person usually counsels from a particular moral viewpoint; if you are to take his or her advice, you should agree in principle with the moral positions of that particular religious community. Also, some persons may find it difficult to take the advice of celibate clergy, because they feel that the celibate has not had similar experiences. In any case, if you decide to seek the wisdom of a priest, rabbi, or minister, make sure that he or she is trained in pastoral counseling, marital therapy, social work, or one of the mental health professions.

Another possibility for advice or therapy is a professionally trained psychotherapist, psychologist, or counselor. These individuals have studied and have been professionally involved in situations such as yours. If the professional is in private practice, such help may be expensive, costing from $35 to $150 per hour; the gravity of your problem must be weighed against the expense. Check first to make sure that the individual is competent and realistic. Look for the recommendations of others. As is the case in other professions, all therapists and counselors are not equally capable. If your finances are limited, you might want to consider a government-funded or nonprofit community clinic.

2. Evaluate your relationship.   If you are serious about preserving and building your relationship, you must analyze it and determine the sore and destructive spots. Look closely. Is your lovemaking perfunctory and dull? Are your communication patterns destructive? Is there no real intimacy or joy between you and your partner? Reading your own relationship is much more fruitful than trying to determine the details of your spouse's relationship with someone else.

It is very difficult to evelute your relationship without the guidance of a professional, since we tend to put blinders over our eyes when it comes to those very areas which are causing the problems. However, we have designed a short test to help you determine whether professional help is, in fact, needed. Decide whether each of the following statements is true or false, and then interpret the results according to the instructions at the end.

1.   I tend to answer questions and solve problems quickly and with little reflection.
2.   We spend less time together now than we did in the earlier stages of our relationship.
3.   Our time together is depressing rather than refreshing.
4.   Sex is less frequent between us than it was last year.
5.   Sex is rarely an enjoyable experience for me.
6.   We both seem to get little affection from the relationship.
7.   We quarrel a lot.

8. Much of the time we are together we avoid talking with one another.
9. We share little besides practicalities of house, money, and children.
10. We don't seem to understand one another.
11. I've had an affair within the last two years.
12. My partner doesn't care for me.

If you have answered "true" to all twelve, you need help, quickly. More than six "true" answers flashes red danger signals. Talk with your spouse and suggest that you both go for professional help. Fewer than six "true" answers means that your relationship is basically doing well but there are some problems in the road that must be tended to. If you have no "true" answers, you probably don't need this book.

3. Change your relationship. Once you have garnered information about the status of your relationship and if you find you are slipping downhill, it is time to move. Change the way you interact with your spouse, or you will no longer be lovers.

It is at this point that confrontation becomes important. The confrontation should not be about your spouse's alleged sexual escapades, however, but rather about the status of your relationship. Confront your spouse with the information you have gathered. Tell him or her that now is the time to take positive steps to improve your relationship, before it is completely destroyed.

Most relationships need outside help to change. Old patterns, especially in long marriages, are very difficult to break. Using a professional marriage counselor usually affords the best chances for improving a marriage. If you feel you both need counseling, yet your spouse will not go with you, you should go for help by yourself. Discuss with the counselor possible ways to bring your spouse into therapy. Often, the fact that you are serious enough to attend therapy sessions will be enough to stimulate your partner to join you.

4. Take charge of your life. When suspicion grows and it finally dawns on you that your spouse could very well be having an affair, you are likely to experience two primary emotional reactions: anger and fear.

Anger is a violent emotion that makes us want to strike out and hit another person because we feel that we have been wronged and hurt.

Even before you are certain that your spouse is having an affair, you may begin to feel betrayed. Francine described the type of anger she felt:

"When I would think about the possibility of Alan having an affair, I could feel myself losing control. Some little thing would happen, and I would go wild. Usually what set off the anger was unimportant, not at all in proportion to the blowup.

"I once bought a lamp I wasn't too crazy about, because the baby had broken the recreation room lamp and we needed another quickly. When Alan got home, he said it was ugly and asked me how much it cost. I told him, and he criticized me for spending too much. It was as if someone had put my hand in a pot of boiling water. I felt hurt and angry and told him to go to hell.

"By that time we were both screaming at one another. Finally, in tears, I stomped up the stairs and into the bathroom, saying to myself, 'I'll bet *she* could do a lot better. Yeah, I'm sure *her* lamp would be beautiful. . . .'"

You may become fearful when you realize that what you've suspected may in fact be true. And then what happens? you think. All my security goes down the drain. What will the future be like? What will happen to me? I'll be all alone. Who will care for me? And fast on the heels of fear chases anxiety, that edgy, nervous feeling that something bad is going to happen and you will be helpless to prevent it.

Anger, fear, and anxiety can freeze you into a deadly inactivity. Instead of rebuilding your relationship, you can subtly destroy it by doing nothing. Also, when you do nothing, you slowly feed a bubbling cauldron of distrust and desire for revenge. Allowed to intensify, anger and fear can give way to full-fledged panic. If you give in to these emotions, you will withdraw, avoid sexual activity with your spouse, and make your shared moments tense and unpleasant.

You must, therefore, take charge of your own behavior and not allow the unknown or the behavior of others to direct your life. You must channel your anger into constructive activity. Focus on the true source of the problem: the condition of your relationship. Set goals for rebuilding your relationship and eliminating destructive attitudes and behaviors. Working toward a goal will help to dissipate your fear of the unknown, and security will come from knowing that you are on a path that will open up new doors, either with or without your present partner. You will have taken your life in your own two hands.

3

Why Affairs Happen

One evening, in the middle of a rather unemotional group session, we noticed that tears were inching their way down Joan's cheeks. Gingerly we asked whether there was something she would like to discuss. She replied in a shaking voice, trying to control her emotion: "If I only knew *why* he had to have her, *why* he had to have the affair, maybe I could have done something to stop it. Then I wouldn't have to be going through all of this."

The question of "why?" is often more a cry of pain than a search for a reason. Even if you knew why your spouse was having an affair, the affair could not be undone. Your relationship, like an egg that has cracked, could never be quite the same again. The wound has been made, the pain will not go away.

Should you, then, search for reasons? Our experience indicates that intellectual knowledge does not significantly change one's feelings; knowing will not take away the pain. On the other hand, knowledge can help us to make sense out of what happened and aid us in restoring order to a chaotic situation. Understanding can lead us to formulate goals for the future, but it can never undo the past. To think otherwise would be to court depression and defeatist attitudes.

Joan continued: "Damn it, for six months I've been blaming myself for his affair, but now I'm starting to see that it wasn't my fault. I kept thinking that it must have been something I did. I kept grinding myself down—like you mash a cigarette butt under your heel—thinking about how rotten I was, how inadequate, and how I deserved to be rejected for the way I was acting. Well, he was acting like an ass too! I had my faults, but so did he. Maybe I should have tried harder, but he could have tried harder, too!"

As Joan realized, looking at some of the causes of affairs may help you realize that just as it takes two people to make a relationship, so also it takes two to end one. In other words, you should not feel that you have been rejected for something that you did or because there is some quality you lack. Accepting this will bolster your self-esteem and prevent self-defeating attitudes and behavior. You should not feel to blame for the failure of your relationship, but you should try to understand where you may have been making mistakes and try to avoid making the same ones in the future.

Who Has Affairs?

The number of people having affairs has been rising over the past decades. Alfred Kinsey's studies in the early 1950s claimed that at least 26 percent of all women—and probably 40 percent—had an affair before they were 40 years old. The statistics for men having affairs were somewhat higher. Kinsey claimed that at least 50 percent and probably 60 percent of men had affairs before the age of 40.

Kinsey's statistics were compiled some thirty-five years ago, before the sexual upheavals of the sixties and seventies. Recent studies, such as the *Hite Report* by Shere Hite (Knopf, 1981) push the figure of married people who become involved in extra-marital affairs to over 50 percent for women and over 70 percent for men.

What type of person has an affair? It was not too long ago that some psychiatrists thought that people who had affairs were mentally ill and that mental illness was the ultimate cause for all infidelity. As late as the 1950s, Dr. Frank Caprio wrote in his book *Infidelity* (Fawcett, 1956) that "Infidelity, like alcoholism or drug addiction, is an expression of a deep basic disorder of character. It is often a symptom of a depression or unhappiness unresolved since childhood." Elsewhere in his book he states that, "Whether conscious or unconscious, infidelity implies the wish to hurt someone else." Various authors have ascribed marital infidelity to immaturity, infantile regression, and hostility toward women. Other words used to explain the adulterer are "sick," "narcissistic," "perverted," "immature," and "deviant."

On the other hand, Drs. Kaplan, Freedman, and Saddock, in their *Comprehensive Textbook of Psychiatry* (Williams and Wilkins, 1980) wrote, "There is considerable question as to whether one man or woman can satisfy all the intellectual and emotional needs of his or her partner and, therefore, whether humans were ever meant to be exclusively monogamous or to mate for life with one partner." In 1954 Albert Ellis wrote (in an article, "Healthy and Disturbed Reasons for Having Extramarital Affairs," in *Extramarital Affairs*) of "healthy reasons for husbands and wives, even when they are happily married and want to continue their marital relationships, strongly wanting and doing their best to discreetly carry on extramarital affairs." And at the farthest end of the spectrum are those, such as the proponents of the "open marriage," who would go so far as to advocate extramarital sex as a life-style rendering fulfillment and serenity.

There are even some people who see the affair as a gift from God. One very religious client told us that God "sent this man to me. He gave him a place in my life in order to bring me joy. It can't be wrong because he comes from God." We heard a secular version of the same story from a male client: "It feels so right. Something which feels so good and gives me such great joy must be part of my destiny."

There is no single "type" of person who elects to have an affair, and different people have affairs for different reasons. Surely, mental illness can be one of those reasons, but we believe that the vast majority of affairs are not the result of a deep-seated emotional problem. Similarly, we cannot blame the Almighty for what is surely an act of free will. On the other hand, we do not see extramarital sex as a positive option for married couples. Too often affairs become destructive and painful for those involved, even when both spouses opt for an "open marriage."

With Whom Do People Have Affairs?

The "other woman" is commonly pictured as a curvaceous 26-year-old siren lying on satin sheets in a black negligee. During the late afternoon hours one might see her out playing tennis or yachting. She is athletic and oh so smooth—laughing, smiling, triumphant. Her lover, or lovers (she's imagined to be quite promiscuous), support her in regal splendor. She eats at only the best restaurants and rides in taxicabs. Bedecked in presents of jewels and furs, she reclines on her white mohair couch and sips champagne.

The "other man" is thought of as oozing with sophistication, a sprinkling of gray at the sideburns, clothes meticulous, the epitome of subdued wealth. He is in a position of power, a man accustomed to success. He stays at luxury hotels, drives a Mercedes, and can converse with equal flair about the opera and high finance.

These popular images could not be further from the truth. According to Melissa Sands, author of *The American Mistress* (Berkley), only 2 percent of women involved with married men are actually supported by their lovers. The remaining 98 percent receive no financial help at all. The "other woman" and the "other man" tend to be very ordinary people who happen to be associated with their lovers through work or social organizations, or because they are neighbors. Contrary to popular opinion, men have affairs primarily with women their own age. Sands points out that 40 percent of the men having affairs have them with women who are within five years of their own age.

Usually, then, the person whom the betrayer chooses is not some irresistible force of beauty, charm, or money, but more often than not the next-door neighbor, the secretary or boss, a friend or colleague. A realistic image of your rival may not make your spouse's infidelity any easier to accept, but at least it will keep you from feeling inadequate or outmatched. Betrayal is grist for the mills of ordinary people.

Types of Affairs

There are different types of affairs, and all affairs do not have the same significance in the life of the person having the affair. Affairs have different functions for different persons. For one person an affair may be a guilt-ridden, heart-wrenching event that affects all those whose lives touch his or hers. For another the affair may be just a passing fancy, not deeply touching his or her life or affecting others.

The least serious type of affair might be called the recreational affair. Consider, for example, two teachers attending a regional education convention, both away from home. They sit next to one another at a session, decide to have lunch together, and feel the heady license of doing whatever they want to do without having to answer to anyone— freedom, at least for today and tomorrow. All the right elements are there: a candle-lit dinner, a subject of mutual interest to discuss (after all, it is a convention), and, especially, the thrill of adventure. They decide to talk some more in her room before going to their separate rooms; within twenty minutes their clothes are off and they end up in bed. After the convention they kiss good-bye and swear to one another never to reveal what happened. Their quick fling hardly fits the definition of what is popularly understood to be an "affair."

The second, more serious, level of extramarital sex leads to deeper emotional intimacy between the two involved. In this case the adulterer enters into a liaison in an attempt, conscious or unconscious, to find something that is lacking in his or her everyday life.

Some of those who have this "supplemental affair" may be looking for friendship, others for excitement. Some may be bored with their everyday lives, others may be fascinated by a pretty face and with the idea of "doing it with another person." This type of relationship can be long-lasting and involve emotional commitment, but the adulterer remains, at least initially, committed to his or her spouse—even though the affair may eventually rupture the marriage. The danger lurking in this type of relationship is that it may escalate into something much more serious than either party may have foreseen.

The third level of extramarital relations is the affair of anger. One client, Susan, described it this way:

"All our married life Max told me what to do, and then every time I did something, even when he had told me what to do, he would criticize me. I wasn't even allowed to cry. His work was always more important than anything I wanted to do. We never talked any more, we rarely went out. I came to hate him more and more. I turned off to sex, and eventually got to the stage where I jerked away when he touched me. The final straw came when I wanted to join a tennis club with some of my friends and he wouldn't allow it. I didn't join, but I wanted to get back at him and I went out and played tennis on my own. And guess what? The first available man I met on the tennis court I had an affair with. And three others followed him. If there had been thirty, I would have taken them all. And I loved it."

In this case the affairs were a symptom of a disease which had affected the relationship between Max and Susan. Their marriage was in very serious trouble, and the affairs were Susan's way of lashing out in anger. In this instance, as is so often the case with affairs of anger, Susan told Max that she was having an affair (actually her fourth!). Max yelled and screamed, called her a whore and a slut, took her credit cards away. She stopped the affair she was involved in at that particular time. The affairs never solved the problems between Max and Susan; they only provided Susan with an opportunity to strike back at Max.

An affair of anger or revenge is a red flag that a marriage needs help quickly, or it will dissolve or condemn its inhabitants to a life of pain and depression interspersed with violent eruptions of anger.

The fourth level of extramarital sexual relations is the replacement affair, when the adulterer is looking for someone to replace his or her spouse. For all practical purposes the primary relationship is gone. The adulterer may be afraid to ask for a divorce, even though he or she has been thinking about it for years. The affair is an act of silent desperation.

Usually, a man having such an affair has already turned his head in another direction and begun a new life. Nonetheless, it may still be very difficult for him to make the final choice, especially if he is prone to feeling guilty. He wonders whether he is making the right decision. If children are involved, he feels that he is deserting them. Consequently, he cannot bring himself to ask for a divorce but rather, by having an affair, attempts to force his wife to make the decision.

We have found that women, on the other hand, tend to be much more direct and realistic. The time span between the initiation of the affair and the request for a separation is often much shorter than that for men, and women seem to experience less anguish than men as the critical moment of decision approaches. Women, in general, are more firm and direct in making their decisions, and our research has also indicated that, contrary to popular opinion, they experience less guilt than men throughout an affair.

Why Affairs?

Our own research has pinpointed three specific causes which lead people into affairs. We will describe those causes here, and we will also go further and describe how you can counteract such causes if you realize that they are affecting your own marriage.

I Feel So Lonely

Our experience and research have led us to postulate that the primary cause of affairs is loneliness, that feeling which develops when intimacy is lacking in one's life. Even though someone may be present and words may be exchanged, there is no true communication.

Many contemporary studies about extramarital sexual activity agree with this assessment. A recent study done by the *Times* of London surveyed over a thousand adults in an attempt to identify the elements of a good marriage. Thirteen factors were listed. The majority of those surveyed responded that communication was the single most important factor in a marriage. Interestingly, while communication was rated the number one factor of the thirteen ingredients for a successful marriage, sexual fidelity was rated as number eleven.

In another recent study, done in the United States by Lewis Yablonsky, almost 50 percent of the men who were having affairs stated that the primary reason for their extramarital sexual activity was the desire for a *relationship* and that sex was only a part of that relationship.

Loneliness should not be confused with boredom. Boredom is a feeling of stagnation that results from a lack of activity. Loneliness, on the other hand, is a yearning for companionship and meaningful communication. It is a gnawing emotion that eats away at our self-esteem. People feel alone when they have no one with whom they share the events, both major and minor, of their lives.

Our group often discussed loneliness. Angela told us of the loneliness a married woman can experience and how it can lead to an affair:

"I had an affair," she admitted, "before I found out about Rick. And now that I think about it, I can understand a little better how he fell into the affair he had. We were both so lonely."

"How did it start?" asked Marilyn.

"Well, one day I was in the bookstore buying material for my dissertation about symbolism in German literature. I was at the cash register holding three or four books, my purse, and a bag of groceries. As I tried to get my wallet out of my purse I started to drop the books. Trying to rescue them, I dropped everything else I was carrying.

"This nice guy behind me jumped down to help me. He picked up the Hermann Hesse novel I was buying and said, 'Oh, you like Hesse?' Turned out he read German also. We talked a little about Hesse, and

I left without a second thought. About a week later I bumped into him in the bookstore again. This time we got into a discussion about German literature, art, politics, you name it. I told him about several books I was using which were out of print, and he asked me if he could borrow some of them. 'Sure,' I told him. 'Stop by the house and pick them up.' He said he would be over about noon the next day.

"He showed up unexpectedly at about ten the next morning. Said he was in the neighborhood and decided to stop by early. He caught me off guard—I was still in my bathrobe. We sat in the kitchen, drank coffee, and talked and talked. It was absolutely glorious! My husband is a news writer, but he gives all his time and attention to his computer when he is home. I could care less about computers. For me, a byte is something you do to a pear.

"We talked for about three hours. I invited him to stay for lunch. The kids were in school, and I hadn't received attention like that from a man for years. He was really concerned about my feelings."

"What happened?" interjected Craig impatiently. "About the sex, I mean?"

"I guess my bathrobe accidentally fell open a little once in a while. That's what he told me afterwards."

"Sure," said Craig, "accidentally."

"That's right, smart aleck, but I must admit that I did notice how interested he became, and I liked that. Rick hadn't looked at me like that for years.

"I knew the kids would be home in about an hour. I told him to wait while I went up to change. Next thing I knew he was up in the bedroom. One thing led to the next. But, honestly, it wasn't just sex. We could sit and talk for hour after hour. Sex isn't everything, you know, Craig. At the time I did not have many friends. I hardly ever saw Rick, and when he and I talked it was never about anything I was really interested in. For Rick I was basically a screwing and reproduction machine. We didn't share much more than that. It was too lonely to bear."

"What happened to the relationship?" asked Marilyn. "Did Rick ever find out about the affair?"

"Nope. We met for about six months more, and after the school year ended he moved to Montana. We decided to end it then. I felt too guilty—didn't think the sex part of it was right. We still exchange

Christmas cards and once in a great while I talk with him on the phone, but it is all very different now."

How Could I Resist?

The second most common reason for extramarital sexual activity is the lure of excitement. After five or six years of marriage, passion may cool, routines become ruts, and the wild excitement of premarital days becomes a fond memory. The once-unfettered couple may now have one or several children. One or both parents may be employed. She cooks the meals and he works around the house. Shopping and temple or church on the weekend. Sex is usually at the same time and in the same way. The feel of one another has become familiar, each other's smell and habits second nature.

One day a new employee appears in the husband's office. She is very different from his wife. His wife is blond, she is dark and mysterious-looking. At a business luncheon they share cocktails; he tells his old stories to someone who has never heard them before. Her breasts swell under her blouse when she takes a breath (he never noticed that about his wife), and she wears a perfume different from his wife's. Their legs accidentally touch under the table. He moves aside, but his heart races a little faster. After several minutes he moves his leg to where he knows she will touch it. This time he does not pull his leg back; neither does she. A mild flirtation. The next time he sees her he fantasizes about undressing her. It's possible, he muses, she might actually let me. In the office he pays more attention to her, and they agree to have dinner together to discuss "some business matters." After dinner, in the car he kisses her and they begin to pet. Soon they are at a motel.

People crave excitement; for some reason they are not content to go for long periods of time without challenging, exploring, or testing themselves. Sometimes this is done vicariously, through such spectator sports as boxing, football, and hockey. Some climb mountains, sky-dive, or race cars for adventure and excitement. When we consider that sexual activity can be one of the most exciting of all experiences, it is no wonder that many people look to a sexual tryst for excitement. The affair combines so many elements of adventure: the tease, the chase, the thrill of discovery, the sneaking, the unleashed passion.

"For eleven years," said a man from Indianapolis, "I thought about other women, I looked at them and undressed them in my mind's eye, I read *Playboy* and *Penthouse*. But I never even considered an affair. I fantasized, even when I was making love with my wife. Once in a while I would flirt, brush up against someone's breast or sneak a little French kiss. Other women really excited me, and I often thought about what it would be like to go to bed with someone other than my wife. Then one evening when I was alone at a party because my wife was out of town, an opportunity presented itself. The woman I was flirting with turned to me and said, 'Oh, your wife's not here. Well, I need a ride home. Maybe we could have a drink or two at my place. Would you like to go now? This dress is a pain and I'd like to get into something a little more comfortable.' At first I could not believe what I heard. I thought she was putting me on, but she wasn't. I was so shocked and frightened that I told her I didn't think I could take her home because my wife was sick and I had to go check on her. Two days later I called the woman from the party. That was it. We had an affair."

Most of us are bored with the everyday rat race. Monotony can sap our energy and leave us limp. Like anemics we feel we need a transfusion of life. A new and attractive face, a mysterious body, the possibility of a wild fling can be very tempting.

All We Do Is Fight

One night Joan told us about the fighting that took place in her marriage:

"I used to get so angry because Hal would never help with the children. He used to walk in the door and flop down on the couch, waiting for supper. I had a job, too, and I felt angry that I was the one who was responsible for the household. I used to scream at him about helping with the kids; it never had much of an effect.

"One Friday he came home, collapsed on the sofa, and asked me what we were having for supper. I had had a horrible day at work, and the children were acting like complete idiots. At first, I did not even reply to his question about supper. I just sat there. 'Well?' he demanded.

" 'I haven't planned anything,' I responded.

"He flew into a rage; I flew into a bigger rage! We started at one another again like we always did. He said some really nasty things and so did I.

"At that point I stomped into the kitchen, took some cold cuts and bread, and went back into the front room. I threw the meat and bread on the floor right next to the couch where he sat.

" 'There's your damned supper,' I screamed at him.

"He jumped up and ran out of the house, yelling, 'I don't have to take this.'

"He told me later, after I found out about his affair, that that Friday night, after driving around for a while, he called her up and asked if she wanted to go for a drink. That night they went to bed for the first time."

Phil told a different story. "When we fought, it was always the same pattern. She would get mad at me for something and then go out and buy clothes. I would get angry and we would yell at one another about money. I think we put all our anger into money. It seemed like we had to fight about something, and money became the most convenient subject to fight about."

"We fought about sex," said Francine. "Alan would get angry because he felt he always had to initiate anything sexual. Which was true—but I usually wouldn't start anything because he was never nice to me during the day. Then he used to pout in bed and roll over on his side. So I would roll over on my side, too. In the morning he wouldn't talk to me. I would ask what was bothering him, but I really knew."

Most couples do not recognize the destructive communication patterns in their life. Each blames the other person. One person attacks and the other defends, then retaliates. They argue and become frustrated. The anger and frustration filter into all areas of their lives, especially the sexual. Many people do not understand that their sexual problems are based on poor communication.

One such couple came to us for therapy.

"We want to find out why we never have sex with one another," he said.

She nodded her head.

"Whenever I want to have sex she has a headache."

"When I want to do something he is busy, or there is a football game, or some damned thing."

"What conclusions have you reached?" we asked. "What did you discuss?"

He looked at us quizzically. "Discuss?"

"What do you usually talk about?"

"Look," he said, "we came in here to find out abut sex, not to talk about talking."

Unfortunately, this couple did not realize that sex is often a barometer of the overall relationship. A relationship is made and sustained through communication, and sex is primarily an intimate form of communication.

Communication can be destructive or nurturing, tearing down self-esteem or building it up. It is easy to slip into destructive patterns of communication that erode your feelings of self-worth and eventually destroy the relationship you would like to foster. People so often try to protect their self-esteem through defensive patterns of communication, but these in turn provoke negative responses that force them to become even more protective. They become caught in a vicious circle.

From a middle-aged mother of four: "He makes me feel so bad. And when I get to feeling bad I become angry. Then I start criticizing. Not that he can hear me; I do it under my breath. But he knows what I am doing and then it just gets worse. I get so frustrated I could just scream."

From a young female lawyer: "I always seem to be giving in. At work I give advice, I'm in charge. Yet at home it seems like he is always right and I am always wrong, regardless of the facts of the issue. I sometimes cannot believe how I'm always saying 'yes, dear' or 'no, dear' just because I'm afraid he'll reject me."

From a male stockbroker: "I keep trying to tell my wife that I need more attention and affection. Sometimes I feel I am almost begging her to touch me. But she just changes the subject and starts to talk about the kids or her friends or the house. I can't get through to her; I feel so helpless and hopeless."

These are examples of destructive patterns of communication into which couples drift. Many times these negative patterns are present in a primary relationship when an affair occurs. We have noted four basic types:

- *Playing the martyr*—trying to protect the little love or security one has by taking the blame for everything that goes wrong in a relationship.
- *Criticizing*—trying to protect one's self-esteem by pointing the finger of blame at someone else.
- *Rationalizing*—finding excuses; placing all sensitive issues in the abstract.
- *Deflecting*—not facing one's experiences and feelings; constantly changing the topic to something less threatening.

Destructive communication patterns inject a poisonous bitterness into a marriage. As each partner experiences more pain, he or she becomes more sensitive and feels more and more rejected. Defenses are built ever higher, huge walls of negative feelings from which steaming cauldrons of anger and abuse are poured down on the attacking partner. Is it any wonder, when communication has become so destructive, that one or both of the partners turn to someone outside of their marriage for love and sex?

Various counselors list other causes of extramarital sexual relations besides loneliness, desire for variety and adventure, and destructive communication patterns, but our research and experience have led us to believe that all other causes can be reduced to one of these three. We do not believe that all individuals who have affairs are in some way mentally disordered or immature, even though neurosis and immaturity can destroy primary relationships and lead to affairs.

In the final analysis we can never be sure what causes a person to leave his or her spouse and seek another partner. We do know, however, that if you eliminate certain destructive elements in your relationships, you can improve that relationship and lessen the chance of infidelity. If you have been betrayed, look to the past, determine whether you and your spouse were locked into destructive communication patterns, and make sure that such harmful elements do not poison your future relationships.

4

Stage One—Betrayed!

The realization that your spouse is having sexual relations with someone else is a devastating, life-changing experience, a betrayal of your trust and commitment. In fact, practically everyone we interviewed felt that the discovery of an affair was the worst experience of his or her life. This feeling of shock and devastation occurs even if both partners feel that there is no longer any love between them, even if the betrayed person has had or is having an affair, and even if one of them has already filed for a divorce.

Almost everyone we have interviewed—the betrayed and the betrayers alike—felt that an affair was a violation of a deep, intimate trust that should be respected at all costs. All seven members of our group felt this way. We have, however, encountered a few people who had had affairs and who felt differently.

"I don't see sex as such a big deal," argued one man. "I like it, I enjoy it, but I don't see where it changes my life. As a matter of fact, I could probably live without it. So what difference does it make as long as I'm discreet and my wife doesn't find out?" A woman client commented, "My commitment is to my husband. That is first and foremost in my mind. If I have sex with someone other than my husband, I keep my mouth shut. Why should anyone else know about it? Marriages break up because people blab. So I do what I want to do, but I am very careful. I want you to understand that I don't do it that much, just once in a while when my home life is getting me down."

In these cases there seems to have been very little emotional commitment to the persons with whom they were having an affair. The secondary relationship seems to have been based on the sexual experience and not on an emotional attachment. For some, the sexual experience might be no more than an afternoon's excitement.

In some instances the person having the affair and even the betrayed one believe that it is possible to maintain two emotional commitments at the same time. (Some couples, upon the discovery of an affair, will turn to "swinging" or "swapping.") This belief, as far as we were able to determine, does not stand the test of time. Usually jealousy and anger enter in and the primary relationship is seriously jeopardized, if not destroyed.

In any event, these cases are exceptions, and they are few and far between. The vast majority of people never forget the soul-shaking experience they had when they discovered their spouse's infidelity. Some never get over it. A few kill or commit suicide because of it.

Those whose spouses are unfaithful are not the only ones who experience the shock of betrayal. Our research showed that a person whose spouse requests a separation or divorce, especially when such a request is unexpected, has very much the same emotional reactions as the person who discovers that his or her spouse is having an affair. Hearing one's spouse say, "I don't love you anymore—I want a divorce," is just as devastating as hearing, "I met someone else—I'm having an affair."

The Mask Falls Away

Through seventeen years of marriage with Carl, Marilyn learned to be a discreet and supportive doctor's wife. But inside her is fire and spirit, as we see in her story of betrayal:

"When I think back now to my discovery of Carl's affair, I imagine myself Anne Bancroft or Gene Tierney—one of those actresses who could look so beautifully wronged. Someone who could stand there tall, shoulders back, eyes glaring and accusing. That kind of confrontation, believe me, needs a long, high-ceilinged room, something with crystal and fire; a room to absorb the tragedy. There was nothing at all graceful when it happened to me. I didn't have the room. It was cheap and dirty, mud and shit that I stepped in and smeared on my clothes.

"We had our separate worlds, Carl and I. He was an orthopedist; he gave papers at conferences and wrote articles. He moved with the men at the university while I raised the children mostly by myself. We belonged to a country club, but he went there only rarely. I worked with the other women on benefits and special dinners. He had his role and I had mine. We both knew our places and life was easy—too easy, I guess.

"Do you know what it's like to see in one moment that the world is not at all what you thought it was, that you'd been mistaken about it for years? There was a mask over my world; at midnight the mask fell away and it was all different. So, you say, this is what it was all the time. That other stuff—the picnics, the doctors' wives' socials, the family vacations, the lovemaking late at night when the kids were asleep—all of that was a sham. I felt so incredibly stupid, so blind, such a fool.

"Oh, there were signs, and I should have known. I found little clues—matchbooks from hotels, unexplained charges on the credit cards, Carl working late, gossip, little catty hints from other doctors' wives— but I couldn't, wouldn't see it. This was the same Carl who'd slept beside me night after night, loving me, maybe, for most of those years together. Then one of those nights he no longer loved me, wanted someone else, loved someone else. And he always looked the same. I didn't see anything different about him."

Marilyn watched her life crumble before her eyes. You build sand castles on the beach, and as long as the sun shines your little village of sand castles is secure. Suddenly, a wave, unnoticed by you, rushes up the beach, then retreats back to the ocean. Nothing is left of your village in the sand. It is as though it never existed. There was no way to stop the wave—you hardly realized it was coming. But your world is completely, forever, and irrevocably changed.

The Sacred Contract Is Broken

Phil, trying to explain his own shock, seemed to plead with the group. "We had an agreement. We promised. Then we were married in church. It was an agreement bigger than both of us. We had a sacred contract."

With love there develops an unwritten contract. This contract is usually an unspoken, mutual agreement made even before marriage vows were said, that two persons will be one. The union is to be exclusive, and that is symbolized by the intimacy of the sexual union. According to this contract, intimate secrets will be whispered to no one else: *I will be faithful and loyal to you, and you will be faithful and loyal to me*. This is the sacred trust two people pledge to one another.

A couple's contract is sanctioned by society when they are given a marriage license and recognized legally as being married. Furthermore, it is guaranteed by an authority beyond the two of them. There is a power—whether it be the power of a superior and guiding society, or the power of a transcendent Being—which certifies the agreement. As Phil said, "It is bigger than both of you."

A couple's world is formed around this unwritten contract: children, house, joint bank accounts. The unwritten contract becomes the foundation for their security. It defines their place in the world. Because of it, they are now seen as a "couple."

Beneath the crushing blow of an affair or the words "I want a divorce," that iron-clad agreement is broken, intimacy and trust are smashed. The betrayed one stands, staring, unbelieving, before the fragments of the relationship.

The Shock of Discovery

Marilyn continued:

"I woke up during the night with a splitting headache and went downstairs to get some aspirin. It was one in the morning. I thought Carl was still watching Monday night football, but the TV was off, and all the lights were out. I went to the kitchen, took the aspirin, and went out on the patio to wait for the aspirin to take effect.

"I heard Carl's voice. He was in the office across from the patio with the window open. His voice was hushed as he talked on the phone, so I could barely make out the words. 'What are you wearing?' I missed some words. 'I could help you take it off.' Laughter. 'I know, Tuesday night. She thinks it's a business trip, an orthopedic conference.' More laughter. 'I love you so much. Sleep well.'

"Suddenly it all made sense. The great awakening. The trips, the matches, the bills, the gossip—everything fit together. 'Oh, my dear God,' I thought, 'please help me.' My body was shaking, and I could hear my voice crying out. My stomach rolled about like a boat in a storm. I remember telling myself to grab hold and think. I thought of the children: I really must check them before going to bed. . . . How stupid, they don't need to be checked anymore, they're not babies. I stopped the convulsive shaking and tried to calm myself a little.

"I remember how clear the night was. I looked up at the stars. So pretty. So far away. The office light went out.

"There's got to be an explanation, I thought. Maybe I didn't hear it right. He wouldn't do that. He loves me. There's got to be an explanation. Maybe we can talk about it tomorrow. No, next week, after I get back from the beach with the kids. There's got to be an explanation.

"All my senses were alive. I heard the crickets. What a grating racket they make. How could such tiny little creatures make so much noise? I concentrated on their chirping, pushing everything else from my mind.

"The wood felt cold under my feet as I walked in, the rug so soft, I had never noticed it was that soft. I met Carl in the corridor.

" 'You fucking bastard! You lying, cheating bastard! How could you do this to us? How could you destroy us?' I punched him in the face as hard as I could. He mumbled something. I spit at him and tried to kick him in the groin. Me, merry little Marilyn. I hurt him, and he got angry. He grabbed at me and got my nightgown instead, and when I tried to run away it ripped off. I ran out in the yard, naked.

"I fell on the grass and cried. I'm not sure how long I was there before I realized I didn't have a stitch on. One doesn't romp through the suburbs in the buff. I went to the door and God damn it if it wasn't locked. I didn't want to go back in anyhow. There I was, naked, madder than a wet hen, and getting cold. I had to do something, so I started next door to Ned and Sally's. Carl must have been watching from the window, because when I started to leave he opened the door and shouted for me to come in. By that time I could easily have killed him. I ran to Ned and Sally's and pounded on the door. They couldn't hear me. I ran over to the flower bed and got some clumps of dirt and threw them at their bedroom window. I can laugh to this day when I think of the look on Ned's face as he peered out the bedroom window, but that night I didn't laugh. I felt like someone had just died."

There can be no preparation for the discovery of betrayal. You may have seen sexual betrayal in the movies or on television. You may have watched your brother or sister or even your parents go through this experience. But that still does not prepare you for the shock when it comes, no more than seeing pictures of a tidal wave prepares you for being smashed and rolled over by a wall of blasting water.

Emotional Phases of the Shock

During the initial discovery—whether, like Marilyn's discovery, an overheard phone conversation, a note found in your spouse's pocket, an anonymous phone call, or having your mate actually tell you about the affair—you immediately pass through five distinct emotional phases:

1. Shock and physical reaction
2. Disbelief
3. A surge of anger
4. A feeling of loss
5. A regrouping of inner forces

Usually the initial process takes about an hour, though some pass through these phases in minutes and for some it may take several days.

1. Shock and physical reaction.   Marilyn's reaction to discovering Carl's affair was a typical one. She experienced the first three phases— shock, disbelief, and anger—very quickly. The shock she sustained was so severe that she became irrational. Usually a shy, modest, introspective woman, she suddenly reacted without control. She became dizzy, her stomach upset; she cried out, ran through the yard nude, and pounded on her neighbors' door. Her rage, as she put it, "took her over for a while." All other feelings became submerged simply because they hurt too much. In a way, Marilyn's reaction was healthy. Like an emotional immunity system, the parts of her that hurt too much to bear shut down, allowing the system to recover; only anger and shock remained, boiling over quickly, impulsively, irresistibly. She couldn't let the destruction happen inside her, so she diverted it: she became the destroyer and struck back.

2. Disbelief.   The betrayed deny what is happening because the reality is too painful to face. As we've seen, they usually deny all the pointers and clues until they meet the fact of betrayal face to face. Although there were plenty of signs for Marilyn, she did not allow herself to read them.

Finally, when the reality is inescapable—as in Marilyn's case when she overheard Carl's conversation with his lover—the denial returns, but now with a different function. Marilyn's self-esteem was so suddenly deflated that she needed some time to gasp, to regain her emotional breath. The betrayed person feels the loss of power, and disbelief is an attempt to regain control, to hold together a world that is suddenly falling apart.

3. A surge of anger.   All of the betrayed we interviewed vividly remembered their anger upon discovering that their spouses were unfaithful. Gerald reacted by raping Marina. Conservative, Catholic Phil tore apart his house in front of his wife and children, smashing lamps and tables and overturning furniture. He tried to kill his employee who was having an affair with Ellen.

The women expressed their rage just as violently as the men. Marilyn physically attacked Carl, spitting at him and kicking him in the groin. Joan spent a great deal of time in denial and rationalization until finally her anger exploded: she destroyed the other woman's car and then physically beat her. Francine turned her anger inward.

4. A feeling of loss.   Almost always, following fast on the heels of anger is a great sense of loss and a deepening sorrow. Marilyn told the group about moving from anger into the final two phases of her initial shock stage: her feeling of loss and the marshaling of her inner forces to meet the challenge:

"We talked the next morning. I was wearing my neighbor Sally's housecoat. Appropriate, wasn't it? The new me.

"When I came into the kitchen, Carl was all dressed, sitting at the table with a cup of coffee. I had that terrible sinking feeling again as soon as I saw him. My first sensation was that of being hit in the stomach. I lost my breath. I looked at him and knew it was true, damn him. He looked so small and puny. I started to feel sick as soon as I asked him what was going on. I told him what I had overheard. I asked him how he could have gotten sucked in by such a cheap, money-grubbing tramp.

" 'No, no,' he answered. 'It's not like that at all. Don't go trying to make it look cheap. She's not a tramp. I *love* her.'

"I hardly heard him; I was nauseous and my head was pounding. I managed to tell him he was a silly old fool, and . . . and . . ."

"What happened?" Francine asked.

"I threw up. I puked all over his shoes.

"After he left for work, the heavens opened and poured rain. I cried and cried. After a while I went and sat in the rec room, and my crying stopped. I had left out a pair of scissors on the coffee table." She paused and blushed with embarrassment, staring at her empty coffee cup. Taking a deep breath, she continued.

"I took the scissors and sliced the hell out of his goddamned chair. His Archie Bunker chair, which was off limits to everyone else; only *he* could warm it." Her eyebrows arched with the word "he."

"She warmed it a little, too, didn't she?" asked Craig.

"Honestly, Craig," said Francine.

"No, he's right," Marilyn continued. "God, I hate her type; one of those phony 'warm' types. 'But she's so warm, she's so *warm*,' Carl kept insisting to me, as if that'd make me understand or like her. 'She's so warm'—made her sound like a damned biscuit or something." She laughed sadly, her eyes misting over. "It's lucky for Carl he wasn't home—it would have been him I sliced. I wasn't thinking straight. Nothing in my whole life has ever made me irrational, not even labor— and I've had three. No, nothing was like this. I'd always been pretty well able to keep myself under wraps. I really exploded this time.

"After the anger I felt so alone. The one person in the world I had really trusted I could no longer trust. I felt . . . not so much as if he had died, but that something had died.

"After I tore up the chair, I started to get my act together. It did me good to get it out of my system. First thing I did was go out and buy a whole lot of clothes, like $3,000 worth, and take a trip. I was trying to make myself look beautiful, and also trying to get back at Carl by spending his money. He spent it on her, I figured, so I could spend it on myself."

5. A regrouping of inner forces.   After discovering the affair, Marilyn flailed about wildly, trying to regain some emotional stability. Following her shopping spree, she even attempted to have an affair—but she felt so bad that she never showed up for the date. Nothing could take away the pain of that initial shock. As Marilyn told us, "Nothing I said or did made a difference—not to him, not to me. Not the clothes, not the trip, not the long, long chats, not making love to him, not calling the whore a whore. . . ."

Marilyn attempted to regain control over her world, asserting herself in contentious and vindictive actions. She did begin to regain some of the power she had lost, but the trauma was still there, imprinted on her psyche, relived in dreams and fought in depression.

Can Trust Return?

Francine, reflecting on Marilyn's experience, summarized a common effect of the initial stage of reaction to betrayal: "The trust is gone. Completely. Even if you want somewhere inside of you to forgive and forget, you can't, because you can never trust again." Often this is true, but it does not have to be this way in every instance. Many rebuild their marriages and form new bonds of trust with their spouses. The rebuilding process takes time and testing, but it is possible and should not be ruled out at this early stage.

Can Sex Return?

Often sex is connected with the initial experience of betrayal. Again, the sexual experience must be seen in the context of the betrayed one attempting to regain some control over his or her mate.

For some, sex at this point is a vain attempt to assert that the contract still exists, and that in some way the betrayal has not taken place or at least does not have the meaning they down deep realize it does have. When Gerald raped Marina in her backstage dressing room, it was a desperate act of anger and domination.

Many betrayed people we interviewed stated that the sexual experience shortly after infidelity is discovered can be wonderful. Both partners try ever so hard: the betrayer, trying to overcome guilt and pain; the betrayed, trying to overcome fear and pain. For others, sex becomes anathema; they find it disgusting and deceitful. Usually sexual activity returns for these persons, too, but at a later stage.

Starting the Cycle Over Again

Once the betrayed person has finished going through the five phases of this first stage, he or she almost immediately begins the cycle over again, starting with phase number two. This time, however, the process is much slower, each phase becoming a stage of development that can last months or even years. Still, fundamentally, the second, more lengthy process is the same as that which took place during the violent moments or hours of the initial shock stage.

If you have been betrayed and look carefully at your initial experiences of the first several days after discovery, then you can almost predict the course of the next four stages through which you will pass. This knowledge can be very valuable, because it can help you prepare for what you must face.

Coping with the Shock of Discovery

One of the most painful experiences a person can ever have is the experience of truly trusting and relying on another person and then having that other person violate his or her trust and reliance at the most intimate level possible. The immediate sensation is that of shock, and after shocks will follow unless checked. Fortunately, as painful as this condition may be, it can be turned around; the process of destruction can be stopped.

Understand your emotions. If you have been betrayed, you are probably still feeling the shock waves, although you may not realize it. This can be true even though the betrayal took place years ago. Discovering betrayal is similar to having an electrical shock run through your emotional system; it numbs the emotions and shocks you into inaction. Understanding yourself and your emotions is the first necessary step in the healing process.

Learn how to cope with your emotions. Understanding your emotions and understanding why a betrayal took place are not the same as *coping* with emotions and betrayal. You must learn new skills and develop new habits. You will vigorously and actively have to take charge of your own life in order to develop these new skills, and as you learn how to implement them you will come to feel better about yourself and those around you.

Expect your emotions to change. Right now you are probably on an emotional roller coaster. That's normal. Don't make quick, irrevocable decisions about your marriage while your feelings are so volatile. If you feel you must make such decisions now, do so in consultation with a counselor or therapist. Keep in mind that as your emotions change you will gain more control over your own feelings as well as your situation.

It is okay to be angry. You will be feeling a great deal of anger. Short outbursts are to be expected at this time. You've been kicked in the head: you deserve to be angry. However, don't wage a war in front of the children—it will only hurt them. Don't harm yourself. Nobody is worth that! It may be helpful to remember that you are not alone: at least one out of every three persons in this country goes through a similar experience. And don't do anything destructive of your spouse or the "other" person. In the long run, this will only hurt you—especially in court, if you both end up there.

Don't threaten your spouse. Threats at this stage usually have the opposite effect of what is intended. There is a place for ultimatums, but they must be thought out carefully and timed correctly, and you must know exactly what you want to accomplish with them. Also, remember that threats can be used against you in court.

Examine why the betrayal took place. You must examine the factors that led to the problems and betrayal. This will also enable you to evaluate clearly the role you may have had in the development of the affair and will help you avoid making the same mistakes again. You will, after such an examination, be better able to choose the direction for which you want to mobilize your resources.

Start preparing for the future. You must set goals for your future life-style and relationships. Do you want to rebuild your marriage? Find another committed relationship? Remain single? Do you want your spouse to leave home? Where will you go if you leave? (Never leave home without first discussing this move with an attorney.) Do you need to see a therapist? Do you have an attorney?

Part of your preparation for the future should include the keeping of a journal of your spouse's activities, in case you eventually decide to take legal action, and a diary that you can use to chart your own personal growth.

5

Stage Two—This Is All a Bad Dream

After the shock of discovery comes denial. If the shock of discovery is like being hit in the stomach and having the wind knocked out of you, then the stage that follows can be likened to panting and gasping to regain your breath. In order to regain control, a betrayed person employs the protective device of denial. He or she simply denies that the unwritten contract has been broken, and so does not have to face the agony and fear inside. At least not for now.

This denial is partly due to the great sense of shame that wells up in a betrayed person: shame at facing others and, most of all, shame at facing oneself.

Everyone in our group experienced an immediate sense of shame. Francine told us: "I wanted to die, I was so embarrassed."

"I felt as bad as you," replied Phil. "I couldn't go back to work. I felt everyone was talking behind my back."

Marilyn stated that she "just stayed home for months. Some of my old friends I never contacted."

Craig said, "I rarely get embarrassed, but this time I felt like someone stole my clothes while I was on the bus."

Joan frankly admitted that she was worried about more than just what others would think: "I felt shame, all right. The twist of the knife, however, was not the shame I felt in front of my family. That was bad enough. But the real shame was the pain of facing myself."

The people we interviewed affirmed that through some paradoxical twist the betrayed take on the guilt for the broken contract. This lies at the root of their shame. "I believed that somehow I must have caused this," explained Joan. "I just could not conceive that I was not somehow to blame."

The betrayed person gradually comes to realize that denial controls the pain only temporarily. And so he or she tries to regain some power by finding an explanation. One evening Francine screamed at the group, "Damn it, I know what happened. Just tell me why. I'm not an idiot. I can understand. There has to be a reason. Why did this happen to me?" The movement from denial to rationalization had begun in Francine. The search for a reason to justify *why* begins to melt away the façade of denial.

Stage two is composed of two different attempts to cope with the initial shock: denial and rationalization. Denial gives the betrayed person a chance to regain some control over reality. Rationalization is an attempt to restore self-esteem.

Denial

Our group spoke often of denial and how stupid and embarrassed they felt when they finally acknowledged what everyone else seemed to have known about for ages.

One December evening, while Francine was describing how she couldn't believe Alan's affair really happened, Phil stood by the window, looking out at the falling snow. Everyone was conscious of his withdrawal from the group and became a little uneasy. Finally Craig turned to Phil and asked, "Something going on in the parking lot, Phil?"

"Nah," Phil said, folding his arms across his chest. "When Francine started talking about denial I went back to what it was like after I found out about Ellen's affair. I tore the house apart at first. I really did." He laughed a little, lost in the reminiscence of his wildness. "Ellen locked herself in our room. I don't blame her. Must have been a real sight. Smashed a couple of lamps, busted a mirror."

Angela smiled. "The Incredible Hulk, huh?"

"Yeah. A few days later, though, I turned back into Mr. Meek and Mild."

"What?"

"Well, I spent the first couple of nights after the crash-a-thon at the shop, sleeping on the beat-up old sofa at the office. Then everything just kind of . . . left me. I felt okay again, even a little elated. Look at how well I'm handling this, I remember thinking. That day I went home after work, regular time, just like nothing had happened. Ellen seemed ready for the shit to hit the fan."

"Bust up the place again, tough guy?" asked Craig.

Phil tossed his head back and ran his fingers through his hair. "Believe it or not, I walked in and said, 'Hi, what's for dinner?'"

"You've got to be kidding," said Joan, amazed.

"Ellen started moving around the kitchen, putting out plates, milk, bread, forks. I picked up the cat and stroked it a couple of times, like I usually do. Ellen softly said, without looking at me, 'How you been? How's everything down at the shop?' When she said that, I felt so . . . relieved."

"You must have been crazy," said Joan.

"No, no," shouted Craig, "it was denial."

"I guess so," continued Phil. "I did feel relieved. When she spoke, everything was the same as always. Nothing different. As if nothing had happened. Life had been good and life was going to go right on being good. The kids would be in soon; life had to go on.

"It was Good Friday and I asked if she had gone to mass. She said no, she was too worried. I asked what she was worried about, and she became very nervous and angry: 'What do you mean? About you! Us! What happened!' I responded that if she was going to receive communion on Easter, she had better think about going to confession. She got all riled up again and said, 'Since when are you so worried about my soul?' "

Phil moved from the window and rejoined the group. "Now I can see what she was getting at, but at the time I couldn't. She thought I was needling her, telling her she was going to go to hell. She was waiting, I think, for me to scream and yell, maybe to hit her. To punish her in some way. All I knew at the time was that life was going on as before and Ellen was in a particularly bitchy mood.

"For some reason I honestly could not believe the affair had really happened, even though I knew it had. It was like there were two parts of me and I kept sliding from one side to the other. One part of me knew what happened; the other part of me did not—or at least this part said it was no big deal. Ellen was my high-school sweetheart. We'd had a big church wedding. She had never been to bed with anybody except me."

"So she said," remarked Francine skeptically.

Phil grimaced. "Leastways not before we got married. I just couldn't believe she'd go five or six times to the Lucky Seven Motel with the guy who drove one of my delivery trucks. Smilin' Sam I used to call him. Now I know why.

"We didn't talk anymore, because the kids began drifting in. 'What's the matter, Mom? You look like you been hit by a truck,' one of them said. 'Stomachache?' asked Karen, our youngest. Ellen had cooked a pot roast. She was a great cook. We all sat around the table, I said grace, and we ate like one happy family."

"God is in His heaven and all's right with the world," chimed in Francine.

"Did you touch her after that?" asked Craig. "I mean, did you go on having sex?"

"Oh, yeah. That went on as usual—even started to get better. But I remember lying in bed a couple of nights afterwards, looking at Ellen sleep. I started to get this ominous feeling, a cold, dark fear that things would never be the same again. She looked so pretty, but she seemed different, other, an object. Still, to this day I remember saying to myself, 'Hell, it's no big deal. We can handle it.' "

Angela straightened up in her chair. "You mean, she never confronted you, made you look at it? She never said, 'Phil, we have to talk about this'? "

"No, not at first. She was waiting for me to do something, I guess."

"But you must have known better," said Angela.

"I blocked it from my mind, but I couldn't block it from my body. My stomach started to kill me the next day. After a couple of days it felt like a five-alarm fire was inside me. Ulcers, I thought. It was worse when I got into bed. I took enough Alka Seltzer to float me down a river, but the pain never went away. I used to sweat with it, it got so bad. Eventually, I started to think about it, to face it. The more I did, the less the pain in my stomach. Doesn't take a whole lot of smarts to figure out what was happening."

Joan laughed. "I got a rash. Lots of itching! Behind my knees, in the crook of my elbow, on my insteps. I remember thinking, in my more lucid moments, Chris is screwing my best friend, having a wonderful time romping in the nude, and I'm here scratching like a monkey."

"For me it was migraines," said Francine. "Like you, Phil, they were worst at night. In bed. They lasted as long as I couldn't talk about the affair."

Phil had an emotional valve that allowed his system to cope with only so much pain. When the burden became so heavy that it threatened to crush him, he simply denied there was a problem. This allowed Phil to regain some control over his emotions. He slowly began to marshal his defenses, until he was able to cope with the reality of Ellen's infidelity, with the shame he felt and his fear of future disruption.

Both the shame and fear attack a person's self-esteem. When Phil escaped shame and fear through denial, he felt a surge of elation. But even in the face of denial the betrayal does not go away. Phil had deluded himself to a certain extent, but he also acknowledged an "ominous feeling," "a cold, dark fear." Yet he pushed these feelings into the background, crammed them back where he did not have to face them.

For many years we have observed how the emotions, especially when not acknowledged, can cause physical reactions throughout the body. Phil's body reacted with an excess of stomach acids and cramps. Joan developed a rash, Francine migraines. Some in the group described recurrent nightmares; others suddenly became clumsy and accident-prone. One man we interviewed backed his car into other cars three times within two weeks. After the third accident, when he got out of the car to check the damage, he tripped in the parking lot, sprained his ankle, and ended up on crutches for five days. "At least it kept me from smashing up more cars in the parking lot," he wisecracked.

The denial stage is short-lived for most people, although they may intermittently slip back to this protective device during the remaining stages.

Some few hold on to denial for a long time, however, often with harmful results. If perception is continually blocked and other, more adequate defenses are not developed, the betrayed person can unleash hidden rage on himself or herself or on others. One woman who had had an affair brought her husband to us. He had begun to drink excessively after he found his wife and the family chauffeur on a blanket behind the bushes in the backyard. He had also begun to gamble—and lose—large amounts of money. His wife wept and pleaded with him in front of us, begging his forgiveness. He patted her on the head and told her she had nothing to apologize for; he said he knew she would never consider making love to someone else.

Some, displacing their hidden anger, abuse their children; others, unable to cope with the shame they feel, totally withdraw from their families and friends and isolate themselves in a protective shell of noncommunication. They may subsequently attempt to break out of their increasing isolation by contacting someone, but then often back away again—much to the frustration of their friends. This is the stage when a betrayed person feels the strongest need for support, but to accept help is to acknowledge the affair. When that acknowledgment would be too painful, the betrayed person is forced to retreat.

Rationalization

Most of those we interviewed spoke of another, more insidious form of denial: rationalization. Those who rationalize do not deny that an affair has taken place, but deny that it has any real significance. Many reasons are proffered to explain how such a thing could have—even should have—happened:

"He is so overworked and has so much to cope with."

"He seduced her; it wasn't her fault."

"He was just feeling low and depressed and needed cheering."

One woman actually told us, "He never gets any exercise and the doctor told him he should!"

When a spouse discovers an affair, he or she experiences an immediate and shattering blow to his or her self-esteem. The spouse's first reaction is often self-defense, which ironically includes defense of the betrayer, because one's spouse is a reflection and integral part of one's own self-image. The betrayed person, by giving reasons, hopes to ease the impact and thus shore up his or her own self-esteem.

Joan's story is a good illustration of this phenomenon. One evening she and Hal had had a small dinner party for some friends and business associates in their fashionable suburban home. She was in the kitchen taking wine from the refrigerator when Hal walked in.

"You certainly are Mr. Iceberg, tonight," she said.

"I've got a lot on my mind. Here, let me help you open the wine."

"Like what?"

"I want a divorce," he said, staring at her. His voice was calm.

She dropped the bottle. Wine spattered her long skirt and gurgled out onto the floor.

Hal did not tell her that he was in love with someone else until six months later.

Joan was able to rationalize Hal's behavior. When she joined the group she hardly appeared to need help, so self-assured and calm.

"You don't *look* upset, Joan. Are you?" challenged Craig.

"Well, I am a little upset, but I think I can understand why it happened."

"Oh, sure," said Craig, "he wanted a lay, that's all."

"No, I really think Hal was going through a mid-life crisis. He's at that age, you know. And he seemed to be awful restless."

"Restless? Don't you mean horny?" asked Francine.

"Besides, he hasn't been as successful in his career as I've been in mine, and I think that always was a problem for him. I overshadowed him."

Craig grinned sarcastically. "And so he decided to overshadow someone else, right? By lying on top of her."

"Let her be, Craig," interrupted Marilyn.

"That's okay, Marilyn, it really doesn't upset me."

"But I'm *trying* to get you upset, Joan," pursued Craig. "Your husband had an affair for over two years, and you act like he had nothing to do with it."

"Well, it's just that I'm not so sure it was totally his fault."

"Joan, no one makes someone else have an affair," said Gerald.

"But there are reasons," she answered. "I can see how it could have happened. We were married young, and Hal had very little sexual experience."

"Got lots now," said Craig.

"Also, because of my job I wasn't around much, and"—Joan coughed and cleared her throat—"she is very pretty. And younger than me. I can understand. He was pulled into it."

"Bet I know what part she pulled him in with," responded Craig.

Francine, exasperated, shouted, "My God, Craig! Why are you giving her such a hard time?"

"Because she is letting herself be bulldozed. Steamrolled. She is sitting here patting him on the head like a little boy, saying 'That's all

right, Mommy still loves you.' I like you, Joan. I like you a whole lot.
That's why I hate sitting here seeing you blind and getting hurt."

Phil addressed Francine: "In a way Craig is right, you know. Joan
should be taking some action." He turned to Joan. "Hal did not just
get a speeding ticket, or forget to pay the rent. He fell in love with
someone else."

"Our sex life wasn't good, I was working too much. Hal still loves
me, I know he does. I haven't lost him. I am not ashamed."

The rationalizer does not really try to understand what happened,
but rather attempts to explain away the affair. Similar to the denier,
who refuses to accept the facts, the rationalizer holds reality at arm's
length. This façade usually crumbles after a short period of time, as
the facts gradually break through the rationalizer's defensive barriers.

Coping with Denial

If you have experienced the shock of betrayal, temporary denial or
rationalization is only natural. Of the hundreds of people we interviewed,
only a handful could not recall having used some form of the defenses.
Denial and rationalization are necessary emotional tools that give you
time in which to gather strength to face what must be faced. Time is
indeed a great healer, and denial and rationalization allow that healing
process to begin.

If you are in this stage now, you might recognize, lurking beneath
the surface, a great fear: the fear of change. Everyone fears change,
especially when we don't have control over the causes which precipitate
it. Right now your whole world is changing: not only the primary relationship in your life but also perhaps your feelings about trust, affection, sex, and sharing. You may have to be responsible for your family
in a way you were not in the past. You may be facing the prospect of
working outside the home for the first time. You may have to face the
prospect of being alone. If you want to rebuild your relationship, you
may be faced with counseling and many other unknowns. In any case,
you will have to face anger and depression.

Any fear that prevents you from accepting change must be gently
moved aside, so that you can take charge of your life and emotions. If
you do not take charge at this critical time, you can very easily be
overwhelmed and hurt. If you find yourself thinking either that the affair

never took place or that it was excusable under the circumstances, consider the following practical steps:

Listen to your body.   The conscious part of your mind may be telling you that everything is under control. "You are doing just wonderfully after all that has happened," you hear your friends say. You know that is not true. Your friends mean well, but their words are not accurate. You feel the pain of violent emotions locked in the fragile prison of your unconsciousness. Listen to your body. When you have headaches, backaches, eye twitches, shaking, tiredness, or flu-like symptoms, it is trying to tell you something. These symptoms are flashing red signs telling you to stop hiding from reality.

Don't withdraw.   You probably feel, somewhere behind your defenses, that you have been made to look like a terrible fool. "Oh, God. Everyone must be laughing at me. How can I ever face my friends again? Everyone's talking about it. I feel dirty." You might even feel too ashamed to ask for help. Not asking for help at such a critical time is like General Custer's turning to his scouts at Little Big Horn, saying, "Don't worry, we can handle this by ourselves."

Now is the time to rely on those support systems you built up and contributed to over the years. Your clergyman or a trained counselor might be an initial step. You might turn to a trusted and discreet relative or friend. It is important that you begin to talk about the affair now and face the changes it will cause in your life.

Be realistic.   Someday you may restore your relationship with your spouse into a trusting, loving union. On the other hand, you may eventually be separated and have to begin a new life. Either way, the fact remains that your relationship will never be the same again. You must be realistic and not try to hold on to something that no longer exists.

Don't use aids to extend denial.   We can try to mask the betrayal that has taken place and thereby extend the denial process in various ways. Angela told us a gripping story about turning to alcohol at one point. When her drinking became an embarrassment to her friends and family, she turned to drugs; first it was marijuana ("so I could feel better about myself"), then Quaaludes and cocaine. "It all happened so fast. My husband and I both began on the drugs. I think we were both trying to run away from the fact that we no longer could be together. One evening when there were no drugs in the house, I punched one of the children. I was almost crazy because there was nothing for me to take and we had no money, and I began to take out my frustrations on the children. That's when I realized I was in trouble."

Move forward.   As we have already seen, when a person has an affair, his or her spouse moves through certain stages. However, it is possible to stall in one of those stages. Becoming mired in the denial stage can be prevented if you take certain steps almost immediately after the discovery/shock stage.

1. Talk to someone—a trusted friend, relative, even the wall if you have to.

2. If possible, calmly begin a dialogue with your mate, even though you might prefer to place your fingers around his or her neck and squeeze tightly. Don't probe and look for details about the affair, but rather discuss the future of your relationship.

3. Begin to reflect on whether it will be possible to rebuild your relationship. Try to look past your anger and fear and think about the future.

4. Obtain data. First, see where your mate stands. Does he or she still profess love and devotion to you? Is he or she willing to rebuild your relationship and work toward a new level of trust? Is there still some room for trust?

5. Get advice from a counselor about handling your emotions and your relationship. It may also be time to get advice from a lawyer as to what needs to be done if the relationship does not work out. Remember, though, that you may be especially vulnerable right now, so any legal advice you receive should be considered soberly. Don't act rashly, and do not let others make your decisions for you.

6

Stage Three—
Please Love Me

About a month after Joan joined the group, she missed several meetings. Then one evening she returned to the group meeting but was hardly recognizable. Much of her face was covered with an assortment of bandages and wrappings and a large bandage stretched across the bridge of her nose, reaching from one ear to the other. Her face was swollen and discolored with various tints of blues and purples.

"My God," exclaimed Craig, "I thought you might be upset after I lit into you several weeks ago, but I didn't think you were that upset. What happened?"

"I decided to improve my looks a little with some cosmetic surgery: a nose straightening, chin tuck, some things like that."

"Oh, Joan," said Marilyn, "I always thought you were so pretty: I would have given my right arm for your face."

"Thanks, Marilyn, but I'm not that pretty. I just thought I'd improve myself a little."

"Yeah," said Craig, rolling his eyes, "and I'll bet you think Hal will love it, don't you?"

"Well, he probably will. He used to tell me I had wrinkles."

"And I'll bet the other woman has a perfect nose, no?"

"Shut up, Craig!" snapped Francine.

"I'm sure you'll look lovely," said Marilyn, trying to calm the turbulent waters.

"Hope I will. I'm trying. One thing Hal's affair accomplished was to shake the shackles off me. I've decided to take charge of my life. I know I have a good job, but I wasn't really trying to improve myself in other areas. So I decided on cosmetic surgery and I bought tons of new clothes. I'm really going to give Hal a run for his money—I'll prove to him that I am the best he can find. Maybe if I had done these things before the affair, Hal might not have gotten involved with someone else."

The pleading stage had begun for Joan. She thought she was going to win Hal back and restore their relationship to some mythical former state of bliss. The other members of the group recounted their pleading stages. "I remember thinking that buying clothes could help make the new me," said Marilyn.

"I tried to get in shape," recalled Gerald, "and because Marina was on campus and hung around with actors, I tried to study drama and went to every play possible."

Francine and Angela both talked about how they tried to win their men back through sex. "I felt like you, Joan," said Francine, "like I wasn't pretty enough. I bought new nightgowns and wore makeup to bed. Our sex life became wild—better than it had ever been before. I was so afraid he was leaving me because I wasn't sexy enough or good enough in bed. I thought that was why people had affairs, because they were looking for sex."

"Would that it were so easy," said Phil.

"I know better now," said Francine.

Fear of Abandonment

Betrayal strips away a person's self-confidence and sense of security. As denial and rationalization are overcome, a betrayed person is overcome by a sickening, panicky fear of abandonment. This fear conjures up childhood nightmares of being abandoned by mother and father, of being lost in a store or left on a bus. Being told you are no longer wanted also rekindles fears of exile hidden deep in our psyches. For primitive man, exile meant death, because one needed the protection, support, and care of the group. The fear of abandonment prowls deep in the recesses of the human spirit. When a person is told he or she is no longer wanted or when he or she discovers a spouse's affair, one of the worst fears possible raises its ugly head: "I'm going to be all alone. No one loves me." As Francine pointed out, "You feel that you are not good enough." You feel that you have failed somehow, that you are inadequate.

Humiliation

Almost everyone in this situation speaks of feeling humiliated. Some say they feel dirty. One 40-year-old blue-collar worker told us that after he had discovered his wife's affair and they resumed lovemaking, he would take long showers and scrub his penis until it became sore. "After being in her I would think of *him* being in her. Then I would try to wash it off me, like she was contaminated." He went on to add that even though he *knew* better, he still *felt* that something of the other man was "left there in her."

Women whose husbands have had affairs feel the same depth of humiliation; they too speak of feeling "dirty," or sullied, by their spouses' physical intercourse with others.

The great paradox of the betrayal experience is the sense of guilt that invariably creeps up and becomes stronger and stronger in the betrayed. Even though the person having the affair or asking for separation is the one precipitating the crisis, the betrayed one increasingly assumes more and more of the blame, feeling shame for his or her perceived failures and inadequacies. He or she apologizes and pleads, cries and makes promises.

To the outside observer it appears that the betrayed is trying to win back the one who has slipped away. "I'll do better. I'll be a great sex partner. I won't fight. I'll win you back. I'll make it better."

But the dynamic can also be seen from a different perspective: in a way, the person who has lost control is making a desperate attempt to regain power. The sense of abandonment results in a great loss of personal power—power over one's emotions, over one's partner, over one's life situation.

This loss of power injures the betrayed person's self-esteem. Our group members spoke of feeling as helpless as a child. "I felt like I couldn't do a damned thing about it at first," said Gerald. "That's why

I struck out at her and tried to attack her. But hitting her didn't work. Even after all of that she still had the power. So I began to ask her not to leave me. I begged her and she said yes, she would stay, and we began to talk. I cried for weeks after that. I felt rotten. Pretty soon I was pleading for forgiveness and apologizing for my faults."

Overcompensation

When faced with abandonment, people try to regain control by convincing their spouses that they are still worthy of love. "I'll change, I'll do anything you want, please love me," is the refrain during this stage. It is a short distance between "She must be giving him a lot of attention" to "I must not have taken care of him," to "I'll take better care of him and give him more attention." The betrayed goes to great lengths to assure his or her spouse that he or she will be better and try harder.

Some get cosmetic surgery and try to change their appearance. Many go on diets to become more sexually appealing. Some housewives feel that they have not been successful enough and try to get jobs. Others become fanatic housekeepers, as if keeping their external environment in order will keep their emotions under control. Many people become hyperactive in this stage and take up jogging or tennis or some other strenuous activity which they think will improve their appearance and make them more desirable.

Communication becomes intense. A couple will often sit and discuss for hour upon hour. They talk about past good times and where the relationship may have gone bad. Causes are sought, promises made.

Togetherness grows as each tries to be loving to the other. Joan told the rest of the group about how she could not even go to the drugstore without Hal's tagging along. "We were always touching each other, trying to reassure ourselves that we were not fearful of the other's leaving."

Practically everyone we interviewed described a great increase in sexual frequency, and experimentation with different forms of lovemaking. Many said this was the best sexual time of their lives. "It seemed like we were screwing every hour on the hour," said one attractive middle-aged redhead. "As soon as he got home from work we would go to bed. Sometimes we would make love on the couch in the front room or in the kitchen. I once got stabbed in the rear by a meat fork on the counter. After that I was a little more careful where I set my rear end when we got passionate."

Some lose their sexual inhibitions in this stage. A woman may think that her husband is having an affair because she would not have oral sex with him. She now throws herself into oral sex. Other couples will experiment with anal intercourse, cross dressing, and sexual aids such as vibrators and X-rated films. One couple we interviewed tried a different approach: after he discovered that she was having an affair, they discussed their past sex life and came to the conclusion that it was boring. Both concurred that they did not want to end their marriage, but she felt strongly that she wanted to continue to have other lovers. She eventually convinced him to do likewise. But both felt that it was a breach of trust and confidence to take lovers behind the other's back; they decided to join a swingers' organization. Eventually, however, their marriage collapsed and they were divorced.

Unfortunately, many counselors and marriage therapists working with such couples will interpret this increase in sexual activity as a good sign and surmise that the relationship is improving. The mistake is compounded sometimes when the couple is told that they have nothing to worry about. This is rarely the case. The determination of whether or not a relationship is improving must be made after the betrayed person enters the final two stages and comes to grips with the anger he or she feels. The betrayed must realize that the sacred unwritten contract has truly been broken. At this stage the couple is making frantic attempts to patch the egg together again. They are overcompensating with sexual activity as in other areas of their lives.

People in the "please love me" stage withdraw from all but a few trusted friends and relatives because of the shame and humiliation they feel and isolate themselves with their spouses. The couple is now intensely concentrating on one another, each with the overriding goal to make the other love him or her again.

Coping in the Pleading Stage

In this stage you have begun to take action. You are now *doing* something. Denial and rationalization froze you into inactivity, providing a defense against the reality. But now you are making something happen. Part of this new activity is increased communication with your partner, and that increased communication includes increased sexual activity. This can provide you with a basis for constructing a new relationship with your mate at a later stage, if you desire.

On the other hand, there are some problems connected with this stage. The pleading stage is similar to the denial/rationalization stage in that perceptions are skewed. The couple still has not accepted the gravity of the situation—that the relationship as it was has been irrevocably shattered. Once the betrayed person realizes that the secure relationship of yesterday is gone forever, he or she can develop coping skills and prepare for the future.

Here are some steps to follow while in the pleading stage.

Be selfish.   First you must focus on your own needs, not those of your partner. That will come later. Do not assume the guilt for what has happened. If you do, then you will focus on your spouse's needs at a time when you desperately need most to care for yourself.

Find a friend.   You need someone to talk with, someone whom you can trust to support you through this crisis. If you do not have such a friend, then go to a clergyman who has some expertise in dealing with these issues, or to a counselor or therapist. Seek someone who can give you sound advice without urging you either to go to war or to give up the struggle. These periods of discussion should be followed by quiet reflection periods wherein you can think through all your options before acting.

Insist that the affair end.   One of your very first steps, if you have not already taken it, should be to insist that your spouse end the affair, if he or she is involved with someone else. Many persons tolerate the affair, at least for a short period of time, probably because they are afraid they will be abandoned if they force their spouses to make a choice, but you should not waver on this issue. If you do, your relationship will probably be over. You must be swift and definite or risk that the feelings between your spouse and his or her lover will continue to grow, eventually swamping your marriage and tipping you out of the boat.

Don't look for causes.   Exploring the past can enrich your personality and help you to rebuild your marriage. However, ultimately it is the present that counts, not the past. The past cannot be changed, modified, or altered in any way. Because there is such a strong tendency to brood over the past in this particular stage, we recommend that you make a strenuous effort not to concentrate on it. Focus on present and future needs.

Don't have cosmetic surgery now. Some people, like Joan in our group, attempt to improve their appearance through surgery. This is a serious mistake. You must realize that no external factors will make you lovable or force your partner to change his or her mind. As a matter of fact, the reason for your mate's affair or divorce may have nothing to do with you! The last thing you need right now is expensive, energy- and time-consuming surgery.

You must take care of yourself, but not in order to win back your spouse. You and your spouse may decide to rebuild your relationship, but such rebuilding will depend upon mutual commitment, exclusivity, and trust—not cosmetic surgery.

Face your fears. This should be a time for quiet reflection, a time to learn more about yourself and to take a closer look at your spouse. You may discover that the person who sleeps in your bed is someone whom you do not really know. Maybe that person has changed over the years and you have not stopped to notice. Possibly you too have changed and have different needs and desires. Quiet reflection undercuts the edifice of fear.

Everyone has fears of abandonment. "What will I do if I am alone?" If you are a housewife you are probably concerned about support. "Who will take care of me?" "Where will I get money?" You might feel panicky. Panic drains your ability to reason and saps your strength. But if you calm down and reflect, you will see that the situation is not as bleak as it at first appears. All states have laws which are enacted to protect both parties. Look into such things as alimony, child support, and your present financial resources. Get a good grasp of what the family income is and what the family's expenses will be in the future, especially as the children grow older. Keep a diary and collect records, in case you have to go to court some day.

7

Stage Four—
How Could You!:
Depression and Anger

Joan had a constant battle with depression after she discovered her husband's affair.

"I'm not sure when I started to let go of blaming myself and started to blame Hal. I guess it was when I began to get really angry. One morning, about three months after I found out about the affair, we started some silly argument in the bedroom. We were just getting ready to go out. I was putting on lipstick and he was tying his tie. He had on a white shirt. I remember cursing at him; then I turned around and smeared my lipstick down the side of his face and all over his shirt.

"He jumped back and said I was crazy. 'You ruined a perfectly good shirt,' he shouted. He said it over and over again. 'How could you ruin a perfectly good shirt?' At that point I lunged at him and smeared lipstick down his suit pants. I started to laugh. I guess he was right—I was a little crazy. Just for a moment, though, I felt some satisfaction. The funny part of it was that we were trying really hard at that time to work on our relationship. We were trying to make a go of it."

"I know when I started to get real angry," said Craig, his face twisted by a little scowl. "It was when I started to think about Sandy and Guy making love together. Somehow I wanted to know all the details. Where did they go? Did they do it in the car? What motel did they go to? Then, when I found out some of the details, I really got mad."

Everyone we interviewed affirmed that they went through a stage of anger and depression. The circumstances may have been different, but the process was the same. After the stage of pleading and trying to please their spouses, their perceptions changed. They became much more realistic. Some developed a much clearer view of their spouses: maybe this other person was not worth all the trouble after all. Others saw their spouses' choices much more clearly and started to shift some of the guilt for what happened from their own shoulders to the shoulders of the betrayers.

Great mood swings occur in this stage. The betrayed at one moment feel liberated, actually elated. The future looks bright, and they can envision trips, new romances (or rebuilding the former relationship), new possibilities. Then the next day they are in the depths of depression. Everything is terrible, nothing is going right. Why live? There is no enjoyment in life, and the road ahead looks incredibly difficult, full of thorns and hardship. They can't seem to get a good night's sleep. They wake up early in the morning, before they want to, feeling frustrated and edgy. The reflection in the bathroom mirror is haggard, drawn, and repulsive.

Tell Me the Details

The betrayed all described a curious phenomenon that takes place in the early days of this stage: they desire to find out everything they can about the affair. They search the house for clues. They question their spouses repeatedly about the smallest and sometimes the most intimate details. And they do this even knowing that those details will stab them in the heart like an ice pick.

As Francine explained, "I not only wanted to know where they went and when, I wanted to know how they made love, whether she was on top. I wanted to know what kind of birth control she used, what color underpants she wore. Did she wear a bra? Did she wear a see-through nightgown? I remember one night after Alan and I had just made love; I was lying in his arms. 'Alan,' I asked, 'I really need to know something.

Did you and Diana have oral sex? I mean, did she do it to you?' He said it wasn't important, he didn't want to talk about it. Finally he admitted they had had oral sex—a lot. I lay there for a couple of minutes and did not say anything. Then—and I didn't even realize I was mad it came so suddenly—I cursed, I cried. I jumped up and went downstairs to sleep on the couch."

We are not sure why people have this insatiable curiosity about their spouses' affairs. Is it to punish themselves in order to relieve some of their guilt? Is it because they cannot quite believe what has happened and need constant verification? Possibly it is one more attempt to make some sense out of what happened. But whatever the reason, the search for more detail leads to an increasing clarity of perception and a more realistic view of what has taken place.

An obsession with details makes the affair a vivid reality and increases the betrayed person's anger. The more a person thinks about what happened, the more hurt and betrayed he or she feels. As the anger wells up inside, so too does depression.

A variation of this intense curiosity also occurs among those whose spouses have abruptly left or asked for a divorce without explanation. In this case, the surprised spouses go over and over past events in their minds and sometimes become obsessed with suspicions about possible affairs. They will ask friends and business associates of their spouses if they have any suspicions, at times going so far as to hire detectives or tail unsuspecting spouses themselves.

Letting Go of the Union

Paradoxically, even as the betrayed become obsessed with actual or imagined details of the affair at this stage, they simultaneously begin to let go of the external union with their spouses. They realize that the egg has truly been cracked and that no one can make a cracked egg whole again. No one can make their relationship like it was before the affair.

Letting go of the marriage situation is not the same as letting go of the other person, which takes longer and cannot occur until the final stage of emotional development after a betrayal. Still, at this stage emotional separation is beginning. It may be that a physical separation has already begun and that you are not living under the same roof, or at least not sleeping in the same bed with your spouse. But up until this point in time you may not have been able emotionally to accept the "separateness" which must eventually occur.

This emotional separation does not mean that the marriage is over or that divorce is inevitable. You may eventually rebuild your relationship and live the rest of your lives together. However, if you are to effect such a reconstruction, "letting go" at this stage seems to be a prerequisite. The reality of the present situation must be accepted. The broken contract must be dissolved before a new one can be formed. But even if it is the case where the relationship has been damaged beyond repair, this stage of emotional separation then becomes the first necessary step leading to a permanent separation.

I'm Furious

Most people who are betrayed have an initial outburst of anger in the shock stage. That initial anger gives way to some form of rationalization or denial in stage two. But anger returns again in stage four, and this anger seems to well up from the very depths of one's being. It normally begins as a feeling of indignation at being mistreated, cheated, and abused. "How dare you to do this to me!" "What have I ever done to you that you should do this to me?" "I'll kill you for the way you are destroying me," are phrases typical of this stage.

We are taught when we are children that anger is bad and that we should not express our anger. This is unfortunate, because anger is a positive emotion that goads you to protect your own sense of self-worth. This powerful emotion is founded on a healthy reaction to what is painful and harmful in your life. Betrayal is a mortal threat to your self-esteem. The anger rising within you is a response saying, "I'm going to take care of myself, I'm going to survive." It is a sign that you are feeling the urge to take charge of your life.

With anger comes the realization that the affair was not all your fault. Your partner may be harming you in a way that you do not really deserve. Anger is the urge to fight back and is used to mobilize energy so that you can protect yourself. Fighting back in this particular instance may mean going to seek the help of an attorney or professional therapist. It may also mean determining your financial resources so you can provide for a separate future. Anger may also impel you to collect data on your spouse's affair. (You may want to hire a private detective—but take this route only upon the advice of an attorney. Never hire a private detective to cause a public spectacle or to retaliate against your spouse or his or her lover.) Anger may also impel you to take care of yourself by searching for future employment and career opportunities.

Unfortunately, anger is also an explosive emotion that can easily run wild, destroying not only the person who feels the anger but others as well. When anger runs rampant it can become rage or fury, which explode in very destructive ways, such as furious retaliation. And retaliation, in the long run, will hurt *you* most.

Some think that retaliation against the person who is involved with his or her spouse will bring that spouse back. We know of an instance where a woman, after learning that her husband was having an affair, went with her girl friend to the suspected lover's apartment and physically beat her, tearing out large clumps of her hair. The betrayed woman's husband, upon learning of his spouse's violent retaliation, became disgusted and angry. He cared deeply for his lover, even though he had no intention of leaving his wife for her, and was devastated by his wife's violence. When they discussed the incident, he became so angry that he spit in her face, spun on his heel, and walked out of the door never to return. The wife's violent action not only landed her in court but drove her husband away permanently and demolished any chances she might have had for a favorable ruling in subsequent divorce proceedings.

Another type of retaliatory action is the retaliatory affair. "If he or she can do it, then so can I." One distraught woman told us, "I'll fix his ass by fixing my own ass!" Unfortunately, that is exactly what happened. When we checked with her at a later date, she reported that she had contracted herpes. Needless to say, she did not get the last laugh. In our research among the betrayed, we encountered many who wanted to have affairs after they discovered their spouse's affairs. Some individuals had as many as five or six affairs within the next several months after discovering their spouses' affairs, and one woman had a grand total of twenty-one affairs within a year. The retaliatory affair is as unproductive as retaliatory violence. In both cases, the person retaliating thinks that some of his or her pain will be relieved. It isn't. Usually the person having a retaliatory affair feels empty and unfulfilled. If you embark on either of these paths, the retaliatory affair, or retaliatory violence, you will only tear down your own self-esteem by doing the very thing for which you have condemned your spouse. Do not jeopardize your future with a rash and hasty action.

Before you take any action at all, first ascertain if the relationship between your spouse and his or her lover is truly a love relationship. It may only be infatuation or a mistake or a passing fancy or an attempt to force *you* to recognize that something is seriously wrong with the marital relationship. Don't allow your anger to overwhelm you and force you to demand a divorce if there is still a chance of salvaging your relationship. Before you get into a definitive separation or demand a divorce make sure that all hope has truly flown out the window. The possibility may still exist that the two of you can restructure your relationship into a satisfying and fulfilling commitment. In other words, don't cut off your nose to spite your face.

Coping with Anger

You can use various techniques to cope with the anger you feel.

Express your anger.   Craig told us during one session that he thought the most beneficial result of his participation in our group was the opportunity to express anger. During one session he exploded in anger—not only at his spouse, but at others in the group as well. The following week he came back and told us, "I can see now, it's okay to get angry, it's okay to let off steam. I feel better. I had kept it bottled up for too long. I wanted to show everyone it didn't hurt that badly. I always had a smart remark or a joke to cover up my own hurt and anger."

Limit your anger.   Sometimes, the top has to be taken off of the boiling cauldron or too much pressure builds up. Most people are brought up in environments where the expression of anger isn't allowed. We were taught that expressing anger was wrong and were made to feel guilty when we "let loose." If you express your anger, either in front of friends or relatives, or by screaming in the woods or pounding a pillow, don't blame yourself. You probably have some very good reasons for being angry.

But if you allow yourself the luxury of feeling and expressing anger, you must limit it. Set a time limit. When you reach that limit, distract yourself with some other activity or thought. Begin planning out a vacation you hope to take when this is all over. Fantasize about lying on a beach and feeling the ocean breeze. Read a book; talk with a neighbor.

Use "self-talk."   One specialist in the treatment of anger, Raymond Novaco, recommends in his book *Anger Control* (Lexington Books, 1975) that you use "self-talk" that will cool you down rather than heat you up. Talk to yourself about other possible ways to handle your problem, empathize with the feelings of the other person, plan out different approaches. Pretend you are a counselor, and talk to yourself about different ways you can reduce stress.

Distract yourself.   You can also distract your anger by becoming task-oriented. Think of things you might do. We knew an engineer who immediately began designing plans for a bridge to span the English Channel every time he felt a useless anger that ran over emotional territory that had already been covered many times previously. Another person went shopping for new clothes whenever she felt that her anger was interfering with her everyday functioning. Expensive, but effective.

Use relaxation methods.   Relaxation techniques can also be very valuable in the treatment of anger. These can be simple, such as contracting and releasing muscles while you focus on your breathing. Other relaxation routines may be more elaborate, such as putting on a relaxation tape or using hypnotherapy. Much is written about ways to relax, and it might be worth your time to explore some of the possibilities most suited to your circumstances and personality.

Depression

There were times when our group would become very somber and we realized a very sensitive nerve was being touched. One such time occurred when the group, which had been meeting once or twice a week for almost three months, was discussing depression and anger. It was late in the evening, and the overall mood of those present had turned almost as dark as the shadows in the corner of the room. Angela had been discussing the downward slide through drugs and alcohol that led to her withdrawal from her friends and relatives. All were listening attentively as she spoke about her struggle with suicidal thoughts. As she continued to speak with great feeling, tears began to streak down Francine's cheeks.

"Did I say something wrong?" Angela asked Francine.

"Not really," responded Francine. "Your story just brought back a lot of feelings I had buried."

"I was beginning to wonder whether you really had a story," said Craig.

"Oh, I have a story all right. But I still hurt so bad. I was so stupid, so incredibly stupid, but at the time I couldn't see any other way out of the swamp. Alan and I used to have a rather violent relationship. At times he would come to bed at night—this was after I found out about his affair—and demand that we have oral sex." Francine's face shaded crimson.

"I never liked it, and after the affair it was practically unbearable for me. I would think of where his . . . his . . . ."

"Penis," interjected Craig.

"Where his penis had been. I envisioned some of her still there, crusted on him. I was repulsed and would pull away, and he would try to force me. The more he would force me, the more I would resist. He would get so angry, he would slap me, and he even pushed me out of bed several times."

"I would have killed him," cried Marilyn.

"I'm not you, Marilyn. I didn't know what to do. I felt so completely helpless. My parents were two thousand miles away on the West Coast, and I had very few friends. It became so bad that I could not sleep without having nightmares. I used to have this dream that I was in the kitchen frying potatoes. Alan was in the kitchen also, smiling and singing. The radio was on in the background playing music. I was frying potatoes in a black iron skillet with a short metal handle. The fire was hot, and when I turned the potatoes some of the grease splashed out of the pan and caught on fire. The whole house is going to burn down, I thought. Frantically, I grabbed the handle of the frying pan. It was red hot. My hand was burning and the flesh, great gobs of it, stuck to the handle of the frying pan. I screamed and cried, and I looked at Alan and screamed for him to help me. He just stood there and laughed. I was in a panic. 'Do something, do something!' He laughed louder. 'You do something. You're in charge of frying the potatoes.'

"Sometimes the dream would vary. Sometimes my clothes would catch on fire, sometimes my hair, or my face would begin to burn. Always there was nothing I could do about it. I would wake up in the middle of the night and feel that I couldn't breathe. I felt chest pains and thought I would surely die. I'd have this tremendous anxiety; sometimes I would jump up in panic, shaking Alan and telling him to call for an ambulance. I felt I wasn't going to make it through the night.

"I began to lose weight and stopped taking care of myself. Meanwhile, Alan continued on with his affair. I still couldn't bring myself to believe it. Every once in awhile I would get a call and a woman's voice would say, 'I'm the one fucking your husband,' or 'He's so good in bed, he loves me more than you.' Then one afternoon the voice said, 'You don't believe me, do you? Look for the scratches on his back when he goes to bed tonight; those are my present.' Sure enough, his back had long red scratch marks. From that point I could not stand the touch of his hand. I would involuntarily jerk away when he would touch me, reacting like someone was sticking me with a needle.

"When we had intercourse I would cry. I would bite my lip to keep from sobbing; it would start to bleed. I stopped going out. I withdrew from the few friends I had; life didn't seem to have much meaning for me. Sometimes I could feel the anger in me and I would lash out violently. I would scream and cry. Once I picked up a coffee cup and hit him in the ear with it. After an outburst the anger would fade and eventually I did not notice the anger, but became more and more depressed. I enjoyed nothing, not even my studies, which I had always enjoyed previously. I had never had a serious job, and I had no idea how I could make any money. What would I do? Where would I go? Who would want me? The more I thought about it the more down I became, and the worse I felt.

"Late one afternoon I was sitting on the bed in my pants and bra, having spent most of the day in bed. I felt completely trapped and helpless. I remember that the sunlight was slanting through the Venetian blinds. My shadow was on the floor, slit apart by the blinds. I looked at my shadow and thought, That's me—broken into a hundred different pieces. I went into the bathroom and filled the tub with warm water. I had heard that it doesn't really hurt if you do it in warm water. I sat in the tub, still in my pants and bra, and cut both my wrists with a knife from the kitchen. I remembered sitting back in the tub thinking, How easy it is; I don't have to fight him anymore. I don't have to be ashamed. I can have some peace. How clear it all is to me now. I remember it so clearly."

Francine's trembling voice finally cracked, and the sobs came. It was the first time she had cried since attempting suicide. The entire group, even Craig, sat quiet for ten minutes. Marilyn held Francine as she sobbed, and Phil placed a hand on her shoulder.

Finally Angela spoke after Francine had quieted. "I was there also," she said.

"Me too," added Craig, "but I felt I had a lot to live for, even though at times I really wanted to end it all."

Francine lifted her head. "I'm still here, but now you can understand why I always wear long-sleeved blouses. I had turned the bathtub faucet on, and I was in such a fog that I never turned it off. It began to drip into the apartment below. My girl friend lived there, and when the water began to come through her bathroom ceiling she ran upstairs. She happened to be a nurse and applied tourniquets. I tried to fight her a little, I remember, and told her to let me go. She never said a word, just dragged me into the bedroom and called the ambulance."

Francine's story is a description of the devastating path of depression. She was thrown into a situation she felt she could not handle. She felt anger and frustration, but like a capped volcano she had no means of releasing the terrible rage burning within. She believed she had no control over what was happening—even over her own emotions, which pushed and pulled at her, buffeting her from every side. The more trapped she felt, the more pleasure drained from her life. She spent so much energy trying to control her feelings that she had few resources for any pleasurable activities. Gradually she lost interest in everything, even in life itself.

If you ask a depressed person what he or she enjoys in life, you will probably receive a blank stare. A healthy person is like a blackboard on which is listed all the pleasures of life. Depression, as it deepens, is an eraser, wiping away more and more of what makes life worth living, until practically nothing is left.

Depressed people find great difficulty in concentrating. They don't even have enough energy to pick up books or magazines which they once found interesting. They no longer go out with friends, and usually their productivity at work slides.

We remember one female medical practitioner who was on the verge of a scientific breakthrough in her particular field of medicine. She had worked intensively on a particular project for eleven months, neglecting her husband and home life to immerse herself in her research. One night when she crawled into bed at 12:30 after a day of work in the hospital and a night of research in the laboratory, her husband exploded.

"That's it!" he cried. "I've had enough, we've both had enough. Your work is more important than me." He angrily shouted at her that he had had an affair for the last three months and that it was her fault.

After the shock subsided and she stopped blaming herself, it was her turn to become angry. What she prized most in her life, her family, had fallen apart. "Why didn't he wait? Why didn't he warn me? I was doing good for others. I was helping to support my family. How could he do this to me?" But the affair was a *fait accompli*. There was nothing she could do.

Her research slowed down, and she spent less and less time in the lab—until she could no longer go there at all. When the results of her research data finally came through, she had no desire even to see the material. She spent whole days in bed. Not sleeping well at night, she felt exhausted during the day. When she did sleep, she would awake trembling and perspiring.

By the time she came to see us, she was crying chronically, had stopped eating, and looked terribly disheveled—hair uncombed, no makeup, and clothes wrinkled. Others took over her role in the biomedical project, and she dropped her position at the hospital. After therapy began, it took almost a year before she settled into residency with another medical institution.

Depression and anger can be found in every stage of emotional development among the betrayed. It is present in the initial shock of discovery and can still be present after the betrayed finally lets go of his or her spouse or rebuilds the relationship in the final stage. But all of those we interviewed mentioned that there was one particular period when they most deeply felt a searing anger intermingled with an almost uncontrollable slip into depression. Many saw this as a most dangerous time because it took such great effort to cope with even the minor chores of daily life. Some felt on the brink of suicide, having lost all power and feeling, so overwhelmed were they by their seemingly hopeless situations.

This stage is normally reached fairly rapidly after the shock of discovery and the stages of denial and pleading. For most, it was about three to six months before they were caught in the alternating tides of anger and depression. This is usually the longest of all the stages and for some it can last for years, crippling their relations with others and sapping their internal strength to cope with job and family.

Depression is a very painful emotion with possibly dangerous consequences. There are certain warning signs you can look for when you feel overwhelmed and suspect depression.

You're not enjoying life.　You no longer enjoy most of the activities you used to enjoy. Your friends irritate you, your job is tedious, your relatives are idiots, and you've given up all your hobbies and pastimes. Sex is boring if not downright unpleasant. Your basic attitude toward life is "Who cares?"

You've been feeling blue for some time.　For at least several weeks you've been crying and just can't seem to "get your act together." The zip has gone out of your life and the sky always seems to be gray and rainy.

You are gaining or losing weight.　Your friends and coworkers have been commenting recently on how much weight you seem to have lost or gained. Your appetite has changed. You either don't feel like eating at all or you can't seem to stop eating.

You never seem to get a good night's sleep.　When you look in the mirror you have that drawn, haggard look about your eyes. Sleep is a real chore. You keep waking up in the middle of the night and you may also be waking up early in the morning with a vaguely troubled or angry feeling. The last thing you want to do in the morning is get out of bed, and sometimes you pull the covers up over your head and hope that the world will go away.

You begin to neglect your physical appearance.　This is just the opposite of the "please love me" stage, when you were very concerned about your appearance and dress in order to win back your spouse. Now you just don't seem to care. It all seems to be too much bother. Who cares how you look anyhow?

You feel like a total failure.　Everything you touch seems to get the plague. You feel that you are to blame for all the misery in your life, but you don't have enough power to change your situation. "If I had been a better lover this would not have happened." "If I lost weight and maybe if I talked more or didn't drink so much there would be no affair." One woman went so far as to tell us, "I pushed to move to California. If we hadn't moved, he never would have met her. Then I insisted that we join the country club, and that's where he met her. I'm only getting what I deserve; it's all my fault."

You feel anxious for no apparent reason.   You sometimes feel that disaster is just around the corner. You are not sure what the disaster will be, but it seems close. You may be waking up in the middle of the night with ominous dread, your heart beating wildly. At times you may feel complete panic.

Sex has lost its appeal.   Not only doesn't sex appeal to you anymore, but at times you can't function correctly. If you are a man, you begin to lose your erection or you are unable to climax. If you are a woman you may "shut down," become nonorgasmic, and even find intercourse painful. We found a number of women who developed vaginismus during this stage of betrayal. This is a condition in which the muscles of the vagina contract during lovemaking, closing the vagina and preventing entrance by the penis.

You may even be thinking of suicide.   You may find yourself fantasizing different ways you could die, with the ominous suspicion creeping up the back of your consciousness that you might want to act out some of those fantasies. We interviewed a severely depressed man who kept a gun in his desk drawer and periodically, as his depression deepened, he would take the gun out of the drawer and set it on his desk. Sometimes he would stare at the gun for over an hour and think about how he could shoot himself, how it would feel to die, and how everyone would feel sorry for him and realize that he had been serious.

These thoughts of death are often a response of anger at oneself and at others, a response confused and addled in the boiling cauldron of depression. Suicide seems to be the ultimate way, at times the only way, to get back at another.

Coping with Depression

Fighting depression is one of the most difficult tasks you may have as you go through the experience of betrayal. Depression comes on as a sneak attack. We want to fight or at least run, but depression pulls our legs out from beneath us. To make it even more difficult, persons who have not experienced depression and have not lived through that numbing experience can't really understand what you are feeling. Some of them try to be helpful with admonitions like, "Pick yourself up by your bootstraps," or "You can get better if you really want to; all you have to do is try." If you take them seriously and come to believe that the reason you are feeling so poorly is because of some lack of effort on your part, you will only become more frustrated, stressed, and, consequently, more depressed.

You probably feel overwhelmed by your problems. The difficulties you have in your life appear to be enormous mountains to climb. "Why struggle?" you may ask yourself.

If you don't take action you will only feel more overwhelmed. But to take action you must *want* to take action. You must *think* action. This means you must first change how you think.

Change your thinking.   Stop looking at everything in black and white. Life is full of grays and other shades. You can't deal in what one of the leading experts on depression calls "absolutist thinking." Aaron Beck of the University of Pennsylvania Medical School sees the depressed person as thinking in absolute terms such as "I am a despicable coward" rather than in more relative and nonjudgmental terms, such as "I am more fearful than most people I know."

The person using absolutist thinking cannot see situations as changed. He would say, "I was such a lousy husband, I'll never be able to rebuild my relationship," instead of thinking, I can always learn some way to handle this, or There is someone who can help me gain the skills I need. Beck counsels a more relativistic and less critical approach to our lives. We have to stop trying to be perfect and be satisfied with the best we can do.

Stop criticizing yourself.   We had a gentleman come to our office complaining that he was never really able to accomplish anything with his life. He felt he was not respected at his job by his superiors and that he was ineffectual as a father and husband. He felt worthless and could not see where he had contributed anything to others or taken charge of his own life. We asked him what he did for a living. He told us he was a vice president of a major steel company. We asked him about his family. He told us he had a devoted wife and three sons— one in medical school and one studying to be a priest. Yet he could see few good accomplishments in his life. He could not even see his partial gains because he focused so strongly on his shortcomings. Many of us do the same.

Examine whether or not you are blaming yourself for what does not go right in your life. Look back over your day and the last week. Think of the bad things that have happened, or the good things that have failed to materialize. Why? Was it your fault? You may find that you are consistently answering these questions with a "Yes, it was my fault." Be aware of how many things you take blame for. Probably you take blame for most of the bad things that happen in your life, if not everything. And even more importantly, you blame yourself because you feel nothing good is happening in your life.

To escape this pattern, try to be as objective as possible. Sometimes you have to step out of yourself and take a careful look at the data. It might help to write down what actually happened. Did you really cause your spouse to have an affair? Are you really such a horrible person? Did your spouse have other alternatives? Did he or she communicate with you? When you study the objective data, you will probably come to a much more balanced picture of your culpability. Beck recommends that you challenge yourself every time you realize the pattern of self-criticism is taking place. Try immediately to think of how you may have positively affected whatever happened. You might reflect on how you can handle the same situation in the future or what skills you might develop to bring about a better result. Remember, if you think of yourself as inept, helpless, and trapped, you will act accordingly, or not act at all. If you think of yourself as positive, powerful, and contributing, you will act in a positive, nurturing way and come to possess that internal power you admire in others.

Limit your feelings of sadness.   You probably have some very good reasons for feeling down and blue. You have been going through a terrible time. Betrayal is a traumatic experience.

Accept your sad feelings—but for only so long. Look around at others you know. You will probably discover that many of them have similar, if not worse, problems. You are not the first person to discover that your spouse had an affair, or that he or she no longer loves you, or that he or she wants to leave you. Close to 50 percent of all couples—living together or married—go through a similar experience sometime in their lives.

Let off steam.   Tell the other person, who is not present, what you want to say. We often did this in our group. Someone who was particularly frustrated or very sad and angry would imagine his or her spouse in an empty chair. Then he or she could scream, yell, and say everything and anything possible to the other imagined person. Marilyn, seething during one session as she yelled at the envisioned image of her husband in an empty chair before her, got up from her own chair, ran to the empty chair, and sent it flying across the room with a vicious kick. "Amazing how much better I feel now," she said afterwards.

Find diversions.   Distract yourself when you feel those uncontrollable thoughts running pell-mell through your brain. Stop what you are doing and take a walk, or pick up something to read. Speak with someone who's close by, or just focus on details in the room or outside. Fantasize about a particularly pleasant scene, such as lying on a warm beach or walking through the leaves on a crisp autumn day.

Avoid the "shoulds" in your life.   We all have little military generals in our heads who lead us around by the nose. These are the "shoulds" and "have tos." They were instilled in us when we were children, and we still conduct our lives according to their commands. "I should be working on my marriage." "I have to lose weight." "I should be acting nicer to John when he comes home." Every "should" and "have to" is a stressor. Each adds weight to the load we already have to carry, making us feel more frustrated and depressed because there are all these things we *should* be doing and can't possibly do.

The "shoulds" make us feel guilty when we don't do them, and this contributes even more to the depressed feeling. They are anxiety builders robbing us of peace and serenity. We pile on the "shoulds" until our life just seems overwhelming. It's just too much.

If you want to eliminate many of the burdens that seem to drag you down, turn the "shoulds" and "have tos" into direct action and plans. Instead of saying, "I really should go see a marriage therapist," say, "I'm going to go see a therapist," or, if that is not realistic at this time you might say, "I don't want to see a therapist at this time because I'm not sure I want to improve this relationship." In any case, don't let yourself be nagged by vague, dictatorial thoughts.

You'll be surprised at how much more you can accomplish and how much smoother life seems to be when you cut out the "shoulds" and begin making direct statements that express your thoughts and desires.

Take care of yourself.   You want revenge against your spouse? Take care of yourself. As Craig told us in our group, "Every kick in the fanny is not a kick in the wrong direction." Your spouse's affair may be just the motivation you need to take hold of your life and grow in ways you may have long desired but never really had that final push to do.

One of the most important actions you can take is to keep moving. Get regular exercise. Join a health club, take up jogging, or begin aerobic dancing. Above all, don't stay in bed and pull the covers over your head. Buy some new clothes and update your wardrobe. Make yourself look good. If you are a woman, invest in a consultation with a makeup specialist; maybe have your hair dyed a color that you've always wanted to try but never quite had the courage to do. Go on a diet and lose some weight.

Make a list of activities you've always wanted to do, but for which you never seemed to have the time. Prioritize the list and pick out the top one or two items. Make plans and take concrete steps to start on those activities. Program some enjoyment and pleasure into your life. Maybe you've wanted to try skydiving or to learn to fly an airplane. What about joining a stamp collecting club or going bird-watching, joining a bowling team or a bridge club? Now is the time to try it.

Stay away from alcohol and drugs.   There is a tendency at this time to try to drown your sorrows in alcohol or to relieve the pain with the quick chimera of drugs. Stage four is the most dangerous time for substance abuse. Alcohol and drugs will not lift the pall of depression or wash away the anger and pain. They will only lead you into more pain. Now is a time when your senses must be alert and your emotions alive.

Use friends and family.   Now is the time to rely on your family and those friends whom you can trust. You will probably notice that many of your friends will avoid you like you have the plague. Don't become depressed by this. It is a natural phenomenon. Your friends are confused. Probably they have been friends with both you and your spouse and may feel a divided loyalty. They may also feel somewhat embarrassed and may not know what to say, so they may say nothing at all. Don't feel hurt if your friends do not call and offer you support. Just thank those who do call.

Stay away from people who will only further depress you. Shouldering others' problems and depressions at this time will make you feel more isolated and burdened than you alrady are.

Remember that you are still lovable.   Just because your spouse has had an affair does not mean that you are not lovable, nor does it mean that you have never been loved. Sit down with paper and pencil and list all of the good qualities you have. You might be humorous, or creative, or pleasant; you could be pretty or handsome, responsible, or talented. You might know how to paint pictures or fix things or be a good student. You may be a good son or daughter or a dedicated employee. These qualities will still be yours whether your spouse is unfaithful or not.

8

Stage Five—
Beyond Betrayal

Angela, after months of depression and confusion and several attempts at suicide, was talking to a friend when she realized that her past life was over and that the time to act had come. "It was as though someone had thrown a switch in my brain," she related. "Time to move, time to make some decisions." The ups and downs of anger and depression that had ruled her emotions for months no longer overwhelmed her. She felt she could finally take charge and do something about her life, especially about her relationship with her husband.

Others in the group described similar experiences: suddenly, after long confusion, they were able to put the pieces of the puzzle together. Above all, they were no longer paralyzed by a fear of what the future might bring. Like Angela, they decided to take charge of the future as best they could, despite some lingering anxiety.

Stage five, then, is decision time, a time for intense introspection, considering options, making choices, and marshaling inner resources to pursue a concrete goal.

We have learned, after years of working with betrayed people, that a betrayed person cannot make important final decisions until he or she is ready. The process cannot be rushed without harmful consequences, and the preparation may take months or even years. The first four stages lead to the point of decision: information is sifted and feelings are analyzed. But no one can push the betrayed to make the final leap.

Where is the turning point? It might be one incident too many, the proverbial straw breaking the camel's back. Marilyn, for example, had tried to rebuild a loving relationship with Carl. She wasn't sure if Carl was still seeing Lisa, but he kept defending her. Finally, when one day he went off to help Lisa get her car started, Marilyn threw in the towel.

The turning point can occur in a simple conversation. You may be discussing something you've thought about many times before, but suddenly it all makes sense and the way to proceed becomes clear. "I had hashed the whole thing over with my friend Becky a hundred times," said Marilyn. "Then one day we were talking and she asked, 'If you were to leave Carl, when do you think you would go?' 'After the holidays,' I responded without thinking. Of course, I thought, I'm going to go after the holidays. It all fell into place; somehow it all became clear."

A move by your spouse that reveals his or her true character may force your decision. Craig might never have made a decision had it not been for his wife and friend urging him to be adventuresome and to "try something new and daring." He did and they did—they swapped—and now they all exchange keys and take vacations together.

For some, the turning point comes in a moment of insight. After months of mulling over possible decisions, Angela saw, "almost suddenly," as she put it, that she could not live with a bisexual husband. For others, the "almost suddenly" decisions may be reached and previewed through the mysterious process of dreams, when their psychic defenses are lowered.

That last push over the hill to a decision is usually perceived by the betrayed as occurring almost spontaneously. "There it was; all at once it was clear," said Francine. "I knew what I had to do. It was the hardest thing I ever did in my life, but I did it. It tore my heart out, but I finally said to Alan one day, 'It's over. That's all, it's over. No more trying, no more apologies.' "

The decision may not always be a decision to leave one's spouse. Often, however, the decision to stay and rebuild one's marriage is more difficult than the decision to leave. Phil and Ellen's relationship took a terrible beating, including a period of separation. She had him followed by a detective, and he threatened her with a lawsuit. Eventually they both decided they wanted one another and did not want to live with anyone else. They still fight, but now they fight fairly and don't run to someone else when feeling hurt or angry.

Making your decision may not always mean taking immediate action, as it did in Francine's case. It may take time to work through your decisions, to study their implications, and plan a strategy for carrying them to completion. Bringing your decisions to a conclusion may take only days, or it may take many months, as it did in Angela's case.

"It was a whole year after I found out about Rick before I made my decision. It shouldn't have surprised me, I guess, that this one man could put me through so much feeling—good and bad. Before Rick, I dated a lot, but I'd only gone to bed with a couple of men. They were nice guys, very attached to me, but sex was something I mostly just daydreamed about. I enjoyed having boyfriends, but something was missing. Then I met Rick.

"I was doing public relations for a company in downtown D.C. when I met Rick for the first time. We got in an elevator together. He was wearing a raincoat and carried a thin leather attaché case. I looked around. The other women didn't seem to be paying him any mind. I couldn't believe it! The dark blond hair swept to one side, the blue eyes, mustache—like Robert Redford. He must have noticed that I was staring at him, because when he got off the elevator he turned and waved at me. I blushed, acted as cool as I could, and smiled.

" 'Who was that?' I asked one of the girls from the building.

" 'Lannigan. News writer on loan.'

" 'Married?'

" 'Nope,' she said, getting off at her floor. She turned to me before the doors closed between us. 'A *definite* nope.' I was a little puzzled by her emphasis on the 'definite.'

"I tried to take the elevator at that same time each day (so did he, I found out later), and we got to be friends. After our first date Rick touched my chin and lightly kissed me good night. This is it, I thought. This is what men are supposed to be like.

"We didn't go to bed for almost a month. I needed time. He knew without asking. Very easy, never an issue, always understood. It was coming, soon, and my blood was purple with it. One Sunday evening, after watching a presidential debate, Rick went to the kitchen, lit a candle, and turned out the rest of the lights. He took the candle back to the bedroom and set it by the bed. I knew then I was staying the night. We didn't say a word. God, how I loved him, having him, slipping away to a place of joy.

"The courtship was whirlwind, and after getting married we quickly had two little boys. We lived in Georgetown, right off Wisconsin Avenue, and did the Washington scene. We made a lot of friends and became very close with Geraldo and his wife, who worked at the Colombian embassy. They would come over and we would discuss international politics. Geraldo would curse the U.S. government and Rick and I would fight about whether Colombian pot should be legalized. It was a happy time—friends, family, the good life.

"I still remember the drizzly Wednesday night I had to fly to Dayton on business. Washington can be ugly during the winter. Rick and Geraldo dropped me and a coworker off at the airport. When we got in the airport we found the flight was canceled, Midwest snowstorm. There aren't a lot of flights to Dayton from D.C., so we figured we would share a cab back to Georgetown and take a morning flight. When we got back to the house on P Street I asked Meg if she wanted to come in for a drink to warm up. 'Sure, why not?' she said. 'Miserable night.'

"As I opened the front door I could hear the stereo. Lights were on, but the place looked empty. I wondered where Rick was and I walked back to the bedroom. The door was open, and I heard voices. I walked in with a 'Hi, I'm . . .' Rick was on the bed, naked, on his hands and knees. Behind him and bent over him, also naked, was Geraldo.

"You have to understand that I loved him, I truly did. And there were the children and the families.

"He cried, pleaded with me, begged me not to leave. He admitted that he was bisexual but swore that he loved me and that he would never do what he did again. I didn't want to leave him. I loved my family, I tried to forgive him. I tried to stay with him.

"But something was destroyed inside of me. I could not get the image of Geraldo and him in bed out of my mind. A crevice split me down the middle.

"We finally separated over a year after I saw Rick with Geraldo. One day I would think everything was fine, the next I was depressed and felt it would never work. I just could not make up my mind until one day after Christmas when I was taking down the decorations. Suddenly it struck me that Christmas would never again be like it was in the past. I cried and felt so very alone. What might have been. All those promises unfulfilled. Still, I recognized what my decision had to be.

"I did love him, though. Even after the separation we would still get together and I would sit in his lap and kiss him. But we never went to bed again."

Angela's story typifies what so many betrayed people feel: a great sadness for "what might have been," for "promises unfulfilled." Long-term sexual relationships begin with a great many hopes, dreams, and plans. When these are lost, and when, in the final stage, that loss is fully acknowledged, a calmness comes over the betrayed. It is the calm of concentration and assurance. You may feel like taking long walks or sit staring out the window, deep in introspection.

"When I finally came to the point of seeing where I should go, I looked back over my past and tried to see where I had come from," explained Phil.

"I could see that the past was over, but I needed to reassess it," added Angela. "When I decided to leave Rick, I didn't just look back on the relationship, I looked over my whole life. I had a lot of decisions to make, a lot of questions to answer: Who was I? How could I have picked a bisexual as a spouse? What was I going to do? Where was I going?"

Looking over the past may also lead to a positive reassessment of the relationship, as it did in Phil's case:

"I never really wanted Ellen to go. I got angry and punished her terribly, but I did not want to drive her away. Sometimes, though, I think she wanted me to drive her away, like the time we had a fight on the Arlington bridge and she threw my wallet into the Potomac. I got so mad I tried to pick her up and throw her over the railing and into the river. The whole scene was so totally absurd that we both started laughing so hard we collapsed on the walk. Soon we were crying and hugging one another. Something had snapped inside of us, and we did not have to hurt each other anymore.

"We had had a lot of good times in the past. There was enough positive there to make us both try to make another go of it. We're back together again, and I think we're a lot better off now."

The decision stage is a time of determination, a time of personal growth through choosing. Self-esteem is bolstered when goals are set and resolutions made. "I knew what I had to do," said Marilyn, "and

I made up my mind to do it, even without knowing where it would lead me. I had no education, no means of support, but I determined that I would make a go of it somehow."

After your decision is made, you will of course need to announce it to your spouse—either immediately or after waiting for some time. Negotiations between you will follow your announcement, and these are usually interlaced with surges of anger.

Overall, then, it is a roller coaster of emotions that accompanies this stage. You will have a sense of calmness immediately preceding and following your decision. But the rest of the time you are apt to be thrown about wildly. You may feel wonderful in the morning and by afternoon be considering jumping off a bridge. One moment hope and possibilities will abound, and the next moment will bring an ominous fear of what the future may bring. A sense of liberation will alternate with a feeling of being overwhelmed by responsibilities.

Sexual activity is often at a minimum during the decision stage. Unlike the pleading stage (stage three), when you may have leaped into fervid lovemaking, this is usually a time of quietude, even during sexual activity. Many have told us that once they'd made their final decisions, they approached sex either as a way of saying good-bye, if that was their decision, or as a way of sealing a new bond of trust with their spouses.

Most people in this final stage also pull back from friends and acquaintances, except for a few close friends and professional helpers with whom they may discuss their decisions and sort out the pieces of their future.

What are Your Options?

All of your choices boil down to three basic options:

1. Rebuilding your relationship.
2. Letting your spouse go.
3. Adopting an alternate life-style.

No one of these options is easier than the others. Eventually you will come to the point of saying, "This is what I must do. I know it. The other two options are impossible."

1. Rebuilding your relationship. This option presupposes, of course, that your spouse has not already left you. If you have found a note on the table and your spouse has disappeared, either to lead a single life or for someone else, you really have no choice. But if you and your spouse are serious and sincere about rebuilding your marriage, then this may be your best option.

Before you choose this option you must first analyze the seriousness of your spouse's commitment and decide whether or not you can build another trusting relationship with this person. Some of the questions at the end of this chapter will help you with your analysis.

This option requires you to work through the pain and anger your spouse's betrayal has caused you. Some people can never get over that betrayal. Never allowing the incident to be buried, they continue to try to punish the other until they destroy their relationship. Choosing this option means forgiving and putting the incident behind you, even though you will never forget it.

You also have to determine whether your relationship was doomed before your spouse ever had an affair. Sometimes an affair is only one symptom of a sickness that has infected a relationship. It may be that your relationship was over before the affair took place.

Taking this option can lead to wonderful results if you and your spouse are sincere in your efforts to change your relationship into a vital, nurturing union. But although it is possible to rebuild a marriage after the discovery of a betrayal, it is far from easy.

2. Letting your spouse go. You may have known that the relationship was in serious trouble before your spouse's betrayal. The affair was not a new disease, but a symptom of a chronic one. You two are actors on a stage closing out the last scene. It is just a matter of dropping the curtain and taking the final bow.

You may also feel that your spouse's affair caused an irreparable breach and that the union you two shared has been split asunder. For you, a violation has occurred that you can never get over. Be aware, however, that many betrayed people who initially think they will never again be able to live with their spouses do in fact come to terms with the betrayal and are able to rebuild their marriages. They never forget the betrayal, but they do learn to live with it.

If, however, you see that your relationship truly cannot be redeemed, this perception is not necessarily a decision in and of itself. It is merely an insight into the true reality of your situation. The hard decision must still be made. If you choose to end your marriage, you must decide to cut the emotional ties that have bound you to your spouse.

It is action on this final decision which becomes a stumbling block for many people. They realize that the relationship is over, but their thoughts obsessively keep leading them back to their spouses. Francine told us: "Every time I got into the car I started thinking about Alan. At times I felt like I was chained to the steering wheel. When I drove I was hardly aware of what I was doing. I would think about Alan. How could he do this to me? Why me? Where did they go? Was she better than me in bed? I hate him." Sometimes this obsession goes on for years. Some people never bring it to an end. They never cut their emotional ties to their spouses, and so they cannot embrace their own lives with all the fears, joys, anxieties, and creativity that go into a new creation.

3. Adopting an alternate life-style.   Some of those who discover their spouses' infidelity proceed to work out some type of accommodation. They learn to live with an ongoing affair and may even decide to take part in the affair, in which case it becomes a menage à trois or sexual threesome. Others, after discussing the situation with their spouses, feel that they do not want a divorce, but that it is unfair for their spouses to be sexually involved with someone else when they are not. And so, with their spouses' acquiescence (they often agree because they feel guilty), they too embark upon affairs.

Craig told us one night about the arrangement he and his wife, Sandy, worked out after he discovered her affair with his business partner and friend, Guy. Craig and Sandy spent a lot of time with Guy and his wife, Beth. They mixed their children and went almost as one family to the mountains in the fall and to Key West in the winter. When Guy and Sandy's affair came to light they suggested swapping as a solution to Craig and Beth.

At first Craig thought the idea was crazy, but eventually he came to a grudging acceptance. "Hell, I didn't want to leave the kids, and Sandy and I had been married a long time. I still loved her. She loved me but said she needed some adventure. Guy and I knew one another since high school. I didn't want to lose him either.

"So I did it. We all talked it out and laid down some rules and I did it. Hell, it made sense—everyone kind of got what they wanted and we're still friends . . . well, sort of friends. It ain't perfect. Don't know how long it will last."

A book published in the early seventies, *Open Marriage* by Nena and George O'Neill, caused something of a sensation when it advocated in glowing language that marriages should be "open" to sexual relations with persons other than your spouse. This utopia is a delicate glass ship most often smashed against the reefs of real emotions, however. Sexual exclusivity is bred deeply into the marrow of our relationships. The discovery of sexual betrayal brings great anguish and the deepest sense of violation to all but a very few. Open marriages, swapping, and swinging are the stuff of fantasies.

How to Choose

Making a decision this important takes serious reflection. The following are some questions that can help you in that process. It is best if you can reflect on them without rushing. If possible, write down your answers and then look at them at a later date before you come to a final decision.

1. What is the level of your spouse's extramarital involvement? Was it a one-night stand, a slip while away from home or after drinking too much? Has your spouse already moved out, torn up your pictures, and returned his or her wedding ring? Has he or she ended the affair and pledged commitment to you? Or are they still seeing one another?

2. Does serious commitment still exist between you and your spouse? Are you helpful and supportive of one another? Do you see an underlying anger in your spouse toward you? Do you feel that he or she does not want to be with you? Can you both express yourselves openly without feeling criticism or rejection? Do you enjoy spending time together?

3. Is your spouse willing to change and sacrifice? Are you? Is your spouse willing to go for professional help from a marriage counselor or therapist or does he or she plead there is not enough time or that it costs too much? Has your spouse pledged to change and professed a desire to make your relationship work? Is he or she making the efforts necessary to improve your relationship? Are you?

4. Are the two of you committed to retaining the unity of your family, whatever the cost? If there are children involved, is your spouse a good parent? Do you function together as a family? Do you take family trips that everyone enjoys?

5. Do you have a nurturing sex life? Is your sex life vital and meaningful? Is your spouse affectionate? Do you touch one another frequently? Do you still kiss one another? Does your spouse cry during intercourse (and not from ectasy), or otherwise indicate a desire not to make love with you? Do you spend extended periods of time in bed together?

6. Do you communicate well? Is there regular fighting now? Do most discussions end with an argument? Is there friction in front of friends and relatives? Was frequent, serious fighting taking place and were you two having difficulty getting along together even before the affair? Do the two of you have similar priorities as regards material possessions, disciplining children, doing household tasks? Do you argue about money?

7. Do you love your spouse and want to grow old with him or her?

8. Can you trust this person again?

If you can answer "yes" to questions 2 through 8, your relationship is strong and chances are excellent that you can rebuild it. Even if you can answer "yes" only to questions 2 and 7, you still have a good chance. Sex (question 5), communication (question 6), and trust (question 8) are areas you can work on and improve. However, if you answered "no" to questions 2 and 7, your relationship is in deep trouble and the healing process will be difficult.

Marshaling Your Inner Resources

Whichever of the three basic options you choose, the fact remains that the primary relationship in your life has changed. The following are some suggestions to help you accept that change.

Face your fears. Those who cannot cope in stage five are those who cannot face their fears. Fear paralyzes and controls us if we do not look it square in the eye and say, "I'm in charge."

Try to imagine the worst thing that could happen in your life. You probably will find, upon examination of this "worst thing," that it is in fact something with which you could live, and that it is not as frightening as it first seemed. Gradually, in this way, you can disarm your fears.

If you plan to rebuild your relationship, you may fear that your spouse will be unfaithful again and that you'll never be able to trust again. If you're going separate ways, you may be afraid you'll never meet another, that you're going to be poor and hungry and lonely, that no one will care for you when you are old.

You may well be able to add more fears to this list. But as you look them over you will come to realize that they all can be avoided, provided you face them and resolve to prevent them.

Expect your life-style to change. The sooner you face this inevitable truth the better you will be able to plan for the future.

Don't rely on external security. Replace your old, worn-out, and unreal security with a commitment to embrace and enjoy life. Life is change and process. You are now in a position to build your own security from within. Whether you stay with your spouse or choose to reject him or her, you will have to depend on your own inner resources in the future.

Define your belief system. Outline your values and priorities. It will help you not only to make your decisions but to live with those decisions in the future. What are your priorities? Is family your highest priority? What do you expect of a marriage partner? Is sexual fidelity absolutely necessary in a partner? If you are religious, should the teachings of your religious community determine your decision? Now is the time to decide what you really believe.

Take time. Serious reflection takes time alone. Walk, get exercise, or just sit with a cup of tea or coffee and think. Do it when your mind is working well—not at eleven o'clock at night after a hard day's work. Read. Many persons turn to more serious books at this time; some turn to poetry. An inspirational book such as *Man's Search for Meaning* by Victor Frankl can help you find your way.

Find a listener. Bounce your thoughts off someone who is willing to listen. That person may be a special friend or a professional counselor, someone you respect and possibly someone who has gone through an experience similar to yours. Discussion groups can also be helpful at this time.

Don't expect an ideal solution.   There is no perfect answer. But remind yourself that your life in the future can and very well could be better than it has ever been in the past.

Evaluate the consequences of your decision.   Try to look into the future and see what results your choices will bring about. For instance, if you are an older woman you may have to resign yourself to the fact that if you leave your husband you may have to live without a man in your life. Statistics show that there are more older women than older men in the world.

If you are planning to rebuild your relationship, you have to consider the possibility that the relationship may not work out. Your spouse may betray you again or you may not be able to communicate.

You may have to get a job in the future if you have not had one in the past. Money may be tight. You may have to take on much more responsibility than you have at present. Unless you are awarded custody of your children, you may not be able to see them as often as you want.

If you decide to leave your spouse, inform him or her first. After you have consulted with a lawyer and taken the necessary legal precautions, it is best to speak with your spouse before anyone else. Do not first inform relatives or friends of your decision, and above all do not tell your children before you discuss the matter with your spouse. Then keep the lines of communication open. If divorce is in your future, the process will be much easier for you if some communication can be maintained.

Not everyone can make the decision needed; not everyone can discard a broken marriage and move on either to rebuild his or her relationship or to let it go completely and leave his or her spouse. Some people can never let go of the past and grow into the future. For them, life becomes a frustrating continuation of unanswered questions. If you find yourself mired in this swamp of indecision, unable to rebuild or let go, you must get help. Individual or group therapy may give you the support and direction you need.

Those who can move through stage five—that is, those who can emotionally release the old and choose the new—recognize the inevitability of change, embrace it, and are spurred on to new possibilities. They will feel the cool, invigorating spring air of liberation.

9

Using Support Systems:
Legal Aid

If you know, or strongly suspect, that your spouse is unfaithful or wants to leave you, read this chapter, then put down the book and phone an attorney for an appointment. At this point in your life what you do not know about the law can hurt you, especially if divorce is a possibility. Are we exaggerating the importance of seeking legal counsel so early—when you first find out about your spouse's affair or desire for separation or even before you are sure about it? Not at all. Appropriate legal counsel can give you much insight and necessary information to enable you to cope better with what is happening. It can give you direction, help you to avoid making mistakes, and clarify your rights.

Attorneys know more than the law. Those who specialize in marital law are objective observers of marital stress. They have an overview of marital situations, which is often clouded for those directly involved because of the great turmoil they are in. A competent attorney will not only help you understand your situation from a legal and financial viewpoint, but will also have the resources to direct you to other kinds of help, such as marriage counselors, psychologists, and psychiatrists.

Many people express concern that seeing an attorney, even for a consultation, means divorce. Men and women who have been betrayed will frequently say, "I'm not really sure what I should do or even what I want and need. Won't I have to follow through and get a divorce if I do see an attorney? Doesn't that move send me down the divorce path?" Absolutely not! Most lawyers are prepared to give you advice in one or several consultations without pressuring you to follow through with a request for divorce. Seeking counsel buys an insurance policy, protection against being taken advantage of, a way for you to take some control over your destiny. It is a precautionary step that could greatly affect your future.

Others are afraid that "if you get legal help you're not only admitting that you are in trouble, but you are betraying a hidden trust and attacking the very person you want to hold close." Phil put it this way:

"I felt that we two were still one. If I got legal aid I was somehow splitting us apart. She took a lot of my money and I almost lost custody of the children because I waited until the last moment. I was afraid. I still hoped that it wasn't going to happen even though I knew I should have gotten my lawyer long before I did."

Retaining an attorney does break down the protective wall of denial, and you may not be ready for that yet. Seeing an attorney about the possibility of divorce means that you have to admit to yourself, and to the attorney, that your marriage has been seriously, and maybe terminally, ruptured. Keep in mind, however, that seeing a lawyer does not create the problem; it merely requires you to face a problem that already exists between you and your spouse.

You may be afraid that your spouse will find out that you have sought the advice of an attorney, and that this might hurt any chances you have for reconciliation. First of all, a meeting with an attorney is regarded as part of the confidential attorney-client relationship. If you are concerned about confidentiality, you can remind the attorney that you regard the consultation as confidential. If you are concerned about the lawyer's bill coming to your home and your spouse seeing it, you can make arrangements with the attorney to pay the bill at the time of the meeting or to have it sent to another address. These concerns can and should be openly expressed to your attorney.

Second, suppose your spouse does discover that you have been seeing an attorney and interprets this as a hostile act. So what? You have every right to be angry. Your spouse's having an affair can hardly be interpreted as a loving act toward you. Maybe he or she should realize that you are angry enough to protect yourself.

Your consultation with an attorney may just shake up your spouse enough for him or her to take you seriously. Your spouse may assume that you will put up with his or her behavior no matter what, and that you will always be there, forgiving, accepting, or at least avoiding. Seeking legal consultation may put you back in a position of control.

Do not let any barriers stand in the way of seeking legal advice and assistance. Don't be defenseless; you should know where you stand, what your rights are, and what action is in your best interest.

Some Commonly Asked Questions about Seeking Legal Help

Why should I see an attorney?   A competent attorney can give straight, objective answers to your questions concerning separation and divorce. Even your closest, smartest friend cannot be completely unbiased in this situation, and when you are facing an uncertain marital future, you need answers from an informed professional. Many men and women who are in marital stress have very unrealistic ideas of the consequences of separation or divorce. An attorney can help you envision future possibilities. A positive, growth-oriented vision of the future is extremely important for you at this time when you need to build your self-esteem and strength. Much of the fear you have might be fear of the unknown, and discussing legal rights and financial matters with an attorney can give you some control over that fear.

Some people consult attorneys without clear knowledge of what they want from them. Sue, for example, was feeling frightened and lonely in her marriage. Her husband had been coming home in the early morning for the past four months. He was unloving and hardly ever talked with her anymore. She asked him repeatedly what was wrong, but he did not respond. Her suspicions grew, and she found more justification for her doubts as time passed. On the advice of a friend she went to see an attorney.

As they discussed the situation, Sue happened to mention that her husband had asked her to sign some "papers" that she did not understand. The papers were a revised deed transferring the family home from joint ownership to the sole ownership of the husband. The attorney realized more objectively than Sue that her husband was probably involved with someone else, and was thinking of leaving his wife. At this point Sue was not really ready to face the ultimate probability of divorce; she focused instead on her rather unrealistic wishes and desires—that is, on ways to win back her husband and save the marriage. Consequently, not wishing to offend her husband she ignored her own misgivings about signing legal documents she did not fully understand. The attorney explained to Sue what she might have been signing, how this would affect her future, what rights she had, and what rights her husband had in this situation. The attorney's clarification had a very sobering emotional effect on Sue.

When a client is erratic because of emotional stress, a divorce attorney can usually be a great help. An attorney is not a therapist and should refrain from counseling on how to handle emotions or on what steps must be taken to rebuild a relationship. However, sensing your fear, confusion, a desire to save the marriage, and the need to save yourself, the attorney will often direct you to an appropriate mental health professional in your community who will suit your needs. The lawyer will only make recommendations; the final decision concerning therapy or counseling is yours. Divorce attorneys are increasingly cooperating and working in conjunction with counselors and therapists to help individuals and couples in marital crisis. Also, your state may have conciliation courts which involve crisis-oriented therapy with the preservation of the marriage as the goal. Such counseling is usually free and can often be accepted by persons who will not or cannot commit to long-range therapy. The attorney you consult should know if this service is offered in your state.

When should I consult an attorney?   You should consult an attorney only if you have *serious* suspicions (if not concrete evidence) that your spouse is having an affair, or as soon as he or she leaves or asks you for a separation or divorce. Do not allow yourself to be defenseless, victimized, without control. You'll only make matters worse if you bury your head in the sand and pretend that all is well. You need to know where you stand and what your legal options are. You need help, support, and advice at this time.

How do I go about finding a good divorce attorney?   Finding a competent divorce attorney is one of the most important tasks facing you at this time. To find one, we advise that you go to several sources in your community and get recommendations. You might tap your local bar association, women's groups, counselors, relatives and friends, or a church or synagogue. There may also be organizations in your area devoted specifically to providing this sort of assistance. Look for listings in your phone book or local library.

After getting recommendations, select three attorneys to interview and assess, preferably attorneys who specialize in domestic relations. While this procedure takes some time and money, in the long run you will save yourself doubts and probably money by making a careful, educated decision about an attorney. Fees for consultations vary. When calling an attorney for a consultation, ask right at the start of the conversation the fee for this meeting and the length of time he or she will give you. Some attorneys do not charge at all for initial consultations, while others charge their normal hourly fee—which can range from $60 to $250. Go with essential questions in hand, ready to determine whether this attorney fits your requirements.

What will happen during an initial consultation? What questions should I ask? A consultation is a meeting with an attorney during which you will be given some general knowledge about the divorce laws in your state and some guidelines for you to follow in your actions. This first meeting will allow you to discuss some of the concerns and questions you have about your own life. It should also give you a feeling for this lawyer's competency, views, and attitudes.

Is the attorney sympathetic to the needs of your sex? Does he or she believe in alimony? If so, under what circumstances? What is the attorney's attitude toward sexual affairs? Is he or she sympathetic to what you have been going through? A good divorce or domestic relations attorney will understand that you are under a great deal of emotional stress at this time. He or she should be able to help you regain control, not act impulsively, and should not waste your time and money by giving you unnecessary data, nor should he or she deviate from his expertise by giving you therapeutic advice, which should be given by a counselor or therapist.

Ask about fees. Find out how much a separation agreement, a contested divorce, and a custody battle for children, if applicable, would cost.

Preparing ahead can save you time and money. Before your consultation write out a brief history of events (use your diary if you have been keeping one). Take this with you and tell the attorney the basic facts. Ask what options you have and what specific actions he or she would recommend and why. Write down the attorney's answers to your questions. Don't be embarrassed to ask the attorney to stop and explain terms or ideas that you do not understand. You are not trained as an attorney and you are paying someone precisely for legal advice on matters which you do not understand.

If you feel that one consultation was not enough, ask for another. Be sure you have all the information you need to determine whether this is a person with whom you want to entrust your future decisions.

Is it important to have a good rapport with my attorney? You are probably going to be "married" to your attorney for at least six months and are essentially trusting him or her with your life. It is, therefore, of the utmost importance that you have a good rapport with this person. There need not be a great attraction between you, but you should feel mutual respect. For instance, if the attorney feels that your spouse has reason to have an affair—because you are not on his or her intellectual level, perhaps, or because you are not a good sexual partner— then you should look for a new attorney. Let common sense be your guide. If you feel too emotionally upset at this time to judge the merits of an attorney, consider bringing with you to the consultation someone you can trust to be objective.

Once I have consulted an attorney, do I have to stay with that person for further legal action? Definitely not. A consultation is only an initial exchange of information, a time to gather preliminary advice from a trained professional. You are not committing yourself to any further dealings with this attorney. If you do retain him or her for your marital problems, you are not committed to use the person for other, unrelated legal matters. Furthermore, you may leave this attorney at any time and go to another, although such a transfer is usually expensive, because initial retainer fees are usually nonrefundable and a new attorney will have to charge you for time he (or she) spends learning about your case and covering ground already covered by a previous attorney. However, if your attorney does not do what was promised, does not return phone calls and is inaccessible, appears to be charging you for unnecessary work or does not appear to be acting in your best interest, fire that attorney and retain another.

Lawyers should be professional enough to know that you need time to consider all possibilities and make the best choices in view of your own personal needs. If an attorney pursues you after the consultation, or makes you feel guilty for taking a long time to decide or for interviewing other attorneys, then go to another attorney.

Should you tell your spouse you are going to see an attorney? Precisely *when* you tell your spouse you are seeking legal advice is important. Most attorneys we interviewed felt that you should not tell anyone that you are seeing an attorney unless and until you become sure you are ready to take further action.

If you tell your spouse prematurely, you can lose significant power and control in the relationship. Knowing that you are seeking legal assistance, he or she could start to hide funds or initiate separation procedures before you are ready, or become much more furtive about the affair. It is extremely important at this time that you use all means possible to maintain some control over yourself and the direction your relationship takes. Remember, you are not yet taking any definite legal action; at this point you are merely gathering data to protect yourself and possibly your children.

It may be that telling your spouse that you are consulting an attorney will cause him or her to take notice that you are not going to allow his or her destructive actions to continue. Your spouse is almost forced to respond when you deliver this information, and that response may be what you really want—though not if he or she replies with great anger. Telling your spouse that you are seeking legal assistance—particularly if you have no concrete evidence that he or she is having an affair but are only relying on your suspicions and uneasiness—could be interpreted as a very hostile act and could cause further estrangement. If your initial impulse is to work on the relationship and you do not intend to move toward a divorce, take extreme caution as to the time of informing your partner that you are seeing an attorney. Carefully think out the possible consequences beforehand.

If you do consult with an attorney, he or she should advise you on telling your spouse about your legal consultation. Even with that advice in hand, however, you still need to think through your decision and do what you feel is best for your particular situation.

What are some of the legal liabilities in having an affair?   Adultery is grounds for divorce in most states. In other words, if you find out that your spouse is having an affair and you decide to divorce, divorce can be granted by the court without your spouse's consent.

An affair can affect the judgment of the court in granting alimony. While a judge does not determine the amount of alimony given to a party based on fault by the other, the judge does take the entire situation into account, including factors such as salary, expenses, and how much has been spent on the affair when determining a final division of funds. Consequently, a wife who commits adultery and is divorced by her husband may still request and receive alimony from her husband.

Child custody cases can also be influenced by the moral and sexual behavior of the parents, since the court has to decide which parent is better able to raise the child.

Should I hire a private detective?   Your attorney may suggest that you hire a private detective if he or she feels that the evidence garnered will be important for the case. As one of our attorney friends stated, "The attorney is the architect of this drama. If he says, 'Hire a private detective,' you should seriously consider hiring a private detective."

If there is a question of how money is being spent in the affair, a private detective may be hired to show where the spouse is spending. This evidence would have bearing on the division of funds. If, for instance, your spouse went to Florida with a lover, or if he or she is spending an extra $500 per month on an apartment that you did not know about, this would have a definite bearing on the case. Your attorney may advise you to keep a diary detailing your spouse's expenses and activities.

A custody battle might develop if children are involved, and a detective's information would be important in this instance. The courts today look at what is in the best interest of the children, which parent would provide the healthiest environment for the children. A private detective could be used to help establish that the morals of the spouse having the affair would endanger the welfare of the children. In one case with which we are familiar, a private detective found that the woman in question would leave her children in the car unattended while she went into her lover's home for sexual activity. This evidence was introduced in court to show that she did not show good judgment concerning the children.

Some people hire detectives because they have an irresistible urge to know what is happening and to identify the "other" man or woman.

This is an emotional need, and this sort of information may not really affect court decisions. If you are feeling the necessity to hire a private detective for these or similar emotional reasons, first consult with your attorney. Make sure you have enough money for your curiosity and make sure the law is not violated.

Hiring a detective cannot hurt you in court (even though it may harm your relationship) provided that the detective does not violate the law. The purpose of the investigation is to gather information in establishing a case.

Private detective fees range from $20 to $100 per hour. Many require an up-front retainer, and you will most probably have to hire one for several days to collect the necessary data.

Can the "other" man or woman be brought into court? For centuries it has been against the law for a married person to have sexual relations with anyone other than the person to whom he or she is married. In the past, bitter spouses could drag lovers into court for what was called "alienation of affection" in order to obtain revenge through the court system. In recent years, the "alienation of affection" law and some of the laws against sex outside of marriage have been taken off the books because they are difficult to enforce and because in the United States marriage partners are no longer regarded as personal property. Therefore, the other man or woman is most often subpoenaed to appear at a divorce trial only for financial and child custody reasons, not because he or she lured the spouse into a sexual relationship. He or she can also be brought into court to testify on specific issues, such as where they went, what they bought, what gifts were given, and so on.

As you can imagine, the emotional stress on the "other" person as well as on your spouse can be severe in these situations. Negative publicity concerning a liaison can be very harmful to a person who is concerned about a public reputation, and the mere threat of revealing an affair in the public forum of a courtroom can be a very powerful weapon if you so choose to use it. An affair does not carry the same stigma of moral turpitude as it did in the past, but don't underestimate the threat of a public revelation.

The threat of a subpoena to make the "other" person appear may be enough to cause your spouse to terminate his or her affair, or it may cause him or her to consider terms more favorable to you in a separation agreement. This often happens in homosexuality cases or if an aberrant form of sexual activity is involved. Despite more tolerant legal judgments and a more liberal attitude in general toward homosexuals, most homosexuals and bisexuals would prefer that their sexual preferences not be exposed in the glaring light of an open courtroom. The spouse threatening to subpoena witnesses under these circumstances has a powerful bargaining card.

However, don't wield this weapon lightly unless you yourself have absolutely nothing to hide from your own past. Also, if you have children, you shouldn't do anything to harm their relationship with their other parent, nor should you besmirch the image of your spouse in their eyes. Also, to destroy your spouse's potential income will hardly benefit future alimony or child support payments to you.

Be cautious, and don't let others or your emotions push you in a harmful direction. Professional and personal lives can be greatly affected by how you handle your decisions at this point. With your attorney and counselor think through every step very carefully to make sure that you are making the best possible decisions, especially if children are involved.

Does seeking the advice of an attorney mean that I am giving up on the marriage?   No. You can, and often should, seek legal help even if you are still hoping to rebuild your relationship. Seeing an attorney indicates that you are trying to find out your rights or liabilities; you are not filing for a divorce. At this stage you are merely obtaining objective information, advice, and assistance.

Our research indicates that men are more apt than women to seek legal advice immediately upon finding out that they have been betrayed, or even when they just suspect betrayal. Women are less apt to think about the business and legal aspects and are more concerned with handling the emotional issues, probably because many women leave finances and legal matters to their spouses throughout most of their married lives. To betrayed women, therefore, we must emphasize again that you need to look at the business aspects of your relationship at this time for your own welfare. No one will take care of you if you do not take care of yourself.

What legal issues must be considered when children are involved?   The courts tend to be very conservative when trying to determine what is in the best interests of the children. In custody battles, evidence of extramarital sexual activity can be used in court when determining the fitness of a parent to properly raise a child. Your attorney will advise you concerning the data you need as evidence and whether or not it would be advisable to hire a private detective to gather data which would establish that you would be better suited than your spouse to have custody of the children.

The court does not automatically consider a parent unfit because he or she has had an affair. On the other hand, indiscriminate sexual activity, exposure of the children to sexual practices, or homosexuality would probably affect the judge's decision. Most judges will rule in favor of what they believe to be in the best interests of the child within a monogamous, heterosexual society.

Custody cases are very traumatic to all involved. Too many custody battles begin because one spouse wants to get back at the other. If you are contemplating a custody battle, be sure that you are taking this course of action because you truly believe that you are better able to raise your children properly. Unfortunately, it is the children who most often are scarred in custody battles.

Does a homosexual relationship affect custody decisions?   The type of sexual affair your spouse has can affect the court's judgment. Although courts normally look upon heterosexuality as more normal than homosexuality, some recent decisions have not considered homosexuality to be a decisive factor in the determination of custody. Your spouse's involvement in a homosexual affair will not automatically give you custody. Also, child support and alimony are not based on fault, but the court does listen and make decisions on all of the evidence that is presented. As stated above, most courts are still conservative when dealing with children and custody.

If your spouse has been involved in a homosexual relationship and you are facing a custody battle, make sure that your attorney is well equipped to handle this type of case and that he or she is sympathetic to your situation.

Should I get a legal separation before filing for divorce?   A legal separation is a contract that spells out the division of money, what payments are due to either or both parties, the division of other property, the custody of children, and visitation rights. You can get a legal separation if you are not ready to get a divorce or if you choose to remain married for legal or religious reasons.

However, most attorneys advise against obtaining a legal separation unless necessary. First, preparation of the separation agreement is costly, and as it is usually a prelude to dissolution or divorce, you and your spouse will probably have to go through another costly legal process for the divorce.

Second, people will usually agree to more lenient terms in a separation agreement because it is not a final settlement. For instance, you may settle for less alimony or child support in this temporary state and plan to obtain more when and if a divorce takes place. But your separation agreement is not final, and it may ultimately work to your detriment. In divorce proceedings the court may look at what you settled for in the legal separation and consider whether it was sufficient for your living expenses. What you settled for in the separation agreement can easily become the final financial terms of the divorce.

The time between a decision to divorce and the actual judgment of the court is a time of anxiety and concern. You may feel great impatience to see some concrete results, to get the matter finished. The separation agreement seems to give results, but real results will come with dissolution or divorce, not legal separation.

If my partner has left me for someone else, how can I be sure I will get financial assistance until the divorce is final? Usually, if the spouse who has left has been the primary wage earner, he or she will offer some financial aid to you and the children, if there are any. If your spouse refuses to help you financially, your attorney can file for temporary alimony and child support. This legal action assures you of a set amount of financial aid paid by your spouse per week or month until the divorce is final. Keep in mind that what you agree to accept as temporary support is often considered in determining the final amount awarded by the court. Your attorney will assist you in determining a reasonable temporary settlement that will work to your advantage in future decisions.

If I leave my spouse, will I be able to obtain financial assistance? Yes. Financial aid is awarded according to need, not fault. The judge is not concerned with who leaves whom at this stage, but awards financial aid in view of who is the principal wage earner and who needs financial aid. The principles stated in response to the previous question concerning the determination of the amount of financial aid requested also apply here.

I know that I want a divorce. What steps should I take? After you choose your lawyer, find out your legal rights, and follow his or her guidelines. (Different states have different laws and procedures.) Should you move out of the marital residence? Should you start putting away money in a separate account unknown to your spouse? Once you are separated, are you still responsible for any future debts incurred? Can you date others before you are divorced? Should you seek employment? Questions such as these can be crucial to your future and should be discussed with your attorney.

Do not act on impulse. At this time you need to work hand in hand with your lawyer. Every action that you take can be used against you, so you need to be very careful. Before any legal action, you generally should not be seen dating anyone. Having sexual relations with another party can be used against you in custody battles. Also, running up large debts or spending money on a boyfriend or girl friend can work against your best interests in divorce settlements.

Plan your finances before you file for a divorce. Have some money put aside to retain an attorney. This fee can range anywhere from $250 to $5,000. The retainer most divorce lawyers require at the onset of a divorce or dissolution is an advance on your account, which will be used for future legal work. Most retainers are nonrefundable, while others are on account and the balance, if not used, is refunded. Ask questions before putting any money down. You are making a financial investment and, as with any investment, you should have all the facts before you act.

You should also have one or two credit cards in your own name to establish credit and write checks. If you do not have a job or career to turn to for emotional and financial support, now is the time to begin exploration. Carefully look over the job market, start talking to your friends about employment opportunities, get catalogues from various colleges and universities in the area. Preparing for the future now can save you years of anguish later.

Some attorneys recommend that the non-wage earner not take on employment immediately, as such a move might cause a judge to award a lower amount of financial aid in a settlement. This could be the case if the marriage was of long duration and the wife was unemployed. On the other hand, an attorney may recommend that even if this is the situation, the wife still might seek employment for her own emotional well-being.

Because divorce can often turn into an ugly battle between two hurt and angry persons, you should try to maintain as much goodwill as possible. Long, acrimonious fights consume considerable amounts of money in legal expenses, and if children are involved the debate can only harm them. Being aware of the pitfalls of angry emotional responses may make the divorce easier for all. It is important you let your attorney know that while you want a fair, just settlement, you wish to do all within your power to keep this process as amicable as possible.

As a general rule, it is best to reach as much agreement as possible outside the courts and outside the attorneys' offices.

How much does a divorce cost and how long does it take?   The average divorce costs between $1,000 and $3,000, with an average time of six months to a year required until all the legal matters are finished. Attorneys usually charge by the hour, but some will also take a percentage of the money awarded to you in a settlement.

If a divorce goes to court—that is, if it is contested and there is a battle over children or money—the fees can run into the thousands of dollars. A custody battle can cost you up to $10,000 or more. Court time for custody battles may run over several days, with each attorney charging $1,000 to $2,000 for each day in court.

Cautions

The vast majority of attorneys are ethical and honestly concerned about doing what is best for their clients. Unfortunately, as with any large group of people, a few are grasping and unethical. Consequently, we must list some cautions.

• Make sure the attorney you choose is experienced in matrimonial law. Marilyn went to an inexperienced attorney who neglected to tell her to keep a financial diary of all the household expenses to substantiate the amount of money her husband was making. She was so emotional during the initial period after the discovery of her husband's affair that planning for her financial future never entered her mind. Today, she is convinced that had she kept this record at the time, her divorce settlement would have been larger. Craig hired an attorney who eventually found that the case was beyond the scope of his abilities; he informed Craig that the case was getting too complicated and that another lawyer should be sought. In both these instances valuable time was lost and money was wasted on unqualified legal assistance. Be careful to check the qualifications and experience of your attorney by calling your local bar association and other attorneys. You might be able to check with other people who have used the services of the attorney you are considering.

• A few unscrupulous divorce lawyers may push you to get a divorce when you are not ready for that step. Some attorneys might not suggest that your relationship could be helped through counseling or that rebuilding the marriage is a viable option, though this may be the case. Those few who are in the profession only to make money may be influenced by the knowledge that they will not make as much from your case if you do not seek a contested divorce. As one prominent divorce attorney told us, "Divorce law is one of the biggest income producers for attorneys. The temptation is sometimes too great and greed overcomes charity."

• You may find yourself infatuated with your attorney, and on occasion attorneys have been known to sexually proposition clients. At this time you may feel vulnerable, frightened, and needy for love and attention. Emotional feelings tend to cloud intelligent, clear thinking and at this time in your life you cannot afford the risk of an affair. If you feel that you are too attracted to your attorney in a sexual or emotional way, change lawyers as quickly as you can. If your lawyer is propositioning you, get another attorney. A lawyer who mixes job and personal life is unprofessional, and this behavior places you at a great disadvantage.

• A divorce attorney may push you to settle the case sooner than you would like or to accept terms that are not right for you in order to collect his or her own fee. Be sure that advice to settle quickly is really in *your* best interest. If you feel uncomfortable about the advice of your attorney, go to another attorney for a second opinion.

• An attorney may suggest that you act in a certain way toward your spouse to speed up the separation or divorce process. Be certain that your actions feel right for you. This is a difficult time to follow your own instincts, and you might like to rely entirely on another person; nonetheless, don't do anything with which you are not comfortable.

Joan and Hal had been separated for several months but Hal was still stalling on child support; Joan wanted full custody and was living in the house with the children. Her attorney suggested that she not allow Hal to see the children until he signed the agreement. Reluctantly, Joan did as he suggested. Hal reacted in anger and desperation. He broke off negotiations and temporarily kidnapped the children, disappearing into another state. In this case the attorney did not properly anticipate Hal's reaction, nor did he suitably take into account possible effects on the children. Joan and Hal possibly could have worked out a solution amicably. Unfortunately, in this particular case any chance at negotiations was dealt an irreparable blow. The divorce was contested at great expense. The only person to profit was the attorney!

- It is possible to spend much more financially on your divorce than you need; some lawyers overcharge or charge for unnecessary services. If you ask questions about charges you can avoid being overcharged, or you may come to realize that you need a new attorney. Ask about the retainer. Is it refundable if you change attorneys? What if you and your spouse rebuild your relationship and you decide not to avail yourself of your attorney's services? Will your money be refunded? One woman wrote us the following complaint:

I was really stupid when I went to an attorney. Boy, I could kick myself. I paid him a $2,000 retainer and he wrote a letter to my husband about a divorce. My husband became frightened and agreed to go for counseling. I dropped the idea of a divorce—and I also dropped $2,000. Would you believe that the lawyer told me that it wasn't refundable and that I should have known that. Was I upset! Believe me, you better find out ahead of time: $2,000 is an awful lot to spend for one lousy letter.

10

Help in Your Community and Religion

Joan told us that the morning after she discovered the truth about her husband's affair, she drove to a nearby church, blinded by tears of rage and pain. Inside the cool, quiet, empty sanctuary she threw herself, sobbing, on the red-carpeted stairs leading to the altar.

"A little melodramatic, wasn't it?" said Craig.

"Not really," replied Joan. "I had always been a religious person and I did not know where to turn. I couldn't really pray then, I couldn't think. I was devastated. I don't know how long I stayed there crying, almost wailing. But it was a place I had gone for help in the past."

"Did it help?" asked Craig.

"Yes and no. I guess I was hoping that somebody—a passerby, a friend, priest, maybe God—anybody, would pick me up, put his or her arms around me, and make it all better. It didn't happen. Exhausted, I left the church and drove home. I felt alone, but not completely alone."

When you have been robbed, you call the police. When you break a leg, you go to the hospital. No one has to tell you to call the plumber when the pipes burst. But the decision to ask for outside help is not so apparent when love and trust are stolen from you, your spirit is broken, and anger and frustration have set off a deluge of painful emotions. Joan cried for help, but most do not.

Because you may not show any outward signs of your pain other than a few dark circles under the eyes from restless nights and too many tears, those around you may not know how badly you're hurting inside. Probably no one will rush up to you and say, "My God, what happened? Let me help you!"

Time will be a great aid to the healing process. Eventually you will work everything out and come to feel better about life. But your progress will be easier and quicker if you accept the help of friends, family, and specially trained individuals and groups who can support you along the way. But you must seek that help. This is no time to be a lonely martyr.

In fact, you are not alone and there is no reason for you to stay hunched in a corner with your problem. You would not be expected to recover your own stolen property, set your own broken bones, or repair faulty plumbing in your apartment. You have every right to ask for guidance and receive assistance for your emotions and problems. But it is up to you to reach out for support.

That in itself can be a problem. At the very least, the experience of betrayal leaves you with scars of mistrust and insecurity. It is easy and sometimes necessary to build a protective barrier of caution between yourself and others.

"I could not even look others in the eyes," said Phil. "Didn't make any difference whether they were friends or the check-out person in the grocery store. I used to think, Do they know? Can they see the hurt? Are they laughing? God, did I feel humiliated. I even started to have lunches alone and leave work early lest I got involved in conversations and someone would say, 'So how's the wife and kids?' "

At worst, you might react by curling up into a ball in the corner and slowly drying into a hard, brittle shell of pessimism and self-pity, unwilling and unable to move, much less to try to ask for assistance. A certain amount of caution is wise, but don't allow yourself to be frozen by fear.

Even if you feel strong and hardy, deciding to get help requires courage. You are taking an important step just by recognizing that you need help.

The next step is talking about the betrayal. Describe and discuss the facts, your feelings, and your fears. Asking for help means you are willing to deal openly with your hurt and to work for your own healing. Asking is not easy, but it is not impossible. Now is the time.

Reaching Out

Relying on Friends

You have made a decision to get outside help. Now what? Send up a flare? A message in a bottle? Who *is* going to help?

If you are suffering the initial shock of discovery, you might first go to that trusted friend, family member, or coworker who will let you unburden yourself, cry, shout—whatever it takes to get your story out. Ask them just to listen to you, no judgments made, no advice given. Sort of an emotional first aid. You need this immediate support in order to function, because an hour later you might have to go to work, grocery shopping, or your child's dance recital. Life is going to go on, regardless of what is happening to you. Sounds cold, but it is true. Unfortunately, no one is going to write you a note you can show the world, "Please excuse————from functioning today. He/she is going through a terribly hard time. I'm sure you'll understand." There are no excuse notes, but there are crutches and helping hands. Use them to get back on your feet so that you can face this problem from a standing position.

Friends are not only for good times. The ancient philosophers centuries ago reasoned that a true friend is someone who wishes you well and wishes good things for you for your own sake, just because of who you are. Good friends, and this includes adult members of your family whom you can call friends, are persons who want to help you when you need the comfort and security of another person. Go to them and lift some of the burden off of your own shoulders.

The best redemption during these times may be sharing food with another. A meal with a friend assures us that we are still worth something, that others care for us, and that maybe we are not so bad after all. If you are not separated from your spouse, go out with a friend to a restaurant. If you are separated, do not wait for someone to invite you over; invite them first.

Rely on friends and family for support, but do not expect them to solve your problems. Friends and family can do only so much. They are probably not trained to handle this problem; even if they were, they are probably not the ones you would go to for professional help.

Not all of your friends and relatives will be able to cope with the situation you present to them. You may share your problem in confidence with someone you trust—a coworker, friend, neighbor, or family member. You may feel a tremendous release as the story is told, tumbling out with all of the tears, anger, hurt, and frustration that have pounded inside your heart and soul. Your confidant may respond with sympathy, a comforting embrace, or total shock and outrage that you have been put through this pain. Perhaps your friend offered advice and assistance. But that friend may not be there for you tomorrow.

Some friends will stand by your side throughout your painful ordeal. But, unfortunately, others, even your closest friends, will turn back to their own lives and problems. Sometimes you may hear the encouraging promise, "If there's *ever* anything I can do. . . ." But experience has proven that this promise to help is all too often well-meant but unfulfilled. You may also feel too proud to call them under these circumstances. You wait for others to call, to offer an invitation to dinner, a night out. But the call never comes and you feel even more depressed.

While the people closest to you will still show their concern, even their interest in your problems may lessen with time. Those around you may soon grow tired of hearing your story. Do not be surprised if you find them avoiding the subject—and you. Especially if you keep re-hashing your problems with them.

Most people would never admit it, but many look upon life as an on-the-spot soap opera. They just love a tragedy, as long as it is some-body else's tragedy. They will ply you for all the lurid details, lead you to tears, gasp and moan appropriately. Then, when they have heard enough, they'll drop you. They have changed channels and you are left bewildered. You bared your soul and you received the quick chill of fading concern in return. Up goes your wall of mistrust.

There are other reasons why friends are sometimes not the best support. Though you might not be aware of it, some of your friends may feel threatened by your experience. You could be an unpleasant re-minder that they might eventually find themselves in the same situation, especially if they are insecure or uneasy in their own relationships.

Friends may also feel divided between you and your spouse. They may have been friends with both of you and care for you both. They do not want to take sides against either of you, so they back away from the dilemma that your very presence creates for them. They avoid you.

Even those who love you dearly, care about you and would sacrifice to take away your hurt, do in fact have their own personal obligations and their own lives to live. You may happen to need their help at a time when they are not free to take care of you, however much they would if they could. The problems that are on your mind every waking minute may not always be on the top of their priority list.

Marilyn told us about how she had turned to her older sister for help. The two had been very close throughout their lives and had often aided one another in times of need.

"Liz and her husband, Tom, were terrific to me at first. I could call them anytime, night or day, and they'd always listen. They lent me money, invited me to go along with them to movies and dinner, and ran interference with our nosy relatives. After a few months, however, I realized I was burning out my strongest supporters. I phoned their house late one night and I could feel the chill in Tom's voice. 'Mar, I've got to tell you that Liz and I have to back off from our relationship with you for awhile. She can't bring herself to say this to you, but I can. We don't have too many free moments any more that are not concerned with Carl's affair and your separation. It's even gotten to the point where we had a fight because I got a promotion in Denver and she's afraid to move and leave you, with the way things are. She loves you, we both do, but she can't live her life and yours, too! Can't you see you're wearing her out?'

"After I mumbled an apology and hung up the phone, I burst into tears, really hurt by what Tom had said. It took me some time to realize that every word of it was true. Liz had been giving me her all, just like when we were kids, and I had been taking and taking without giving much in return. I knew she had her own worries, but I couldn't remember the last time I'd even asked about what was happening in her life."

Fortunately, Marilyn and her sister worked through their problems and are still close friends, even though Liz and Tom did move to Denver. When the time came for Marilyn to look somewhere else for advice and support, she luckily had a boot in the right direction. She came in for counseling sessions and joined a separated and divorced group which met at her church instead of relying almost totally on her sister.

We can picture anyone's mother throwing up her hands in despair, crying, "What? At a time like this, you want to take your troubles to strangers?" But sometimes your parents, your big brother, or your favorite aunt doesn't know the best advice to give you—not because they don't love you, but because they are not skilled in handling the complex problems of your situation. They probably have not gone through what you are going through, and they have difficulty resonating with the emotions you are feeling. Members of your own family may have hurt feelings of their own to nurse if your spouse was an active part of the family circle. They may feel that their trust, too, has been betrayed, and their emotional reaction could keep them from giving you sound, unbiased advice.

If you've felt comfortable in the past sharing your personal problems with your family, you will probably welcome their loving concern during this crisis. But you may not feel safe revealing everything about your relationship with your spouse and all the details of the betrayal. You are probably better off accepting your family's sympathy, hugs, and tears, and then going to "strangers"—that is, to trained, qualified professionals and experienced groups—for practical and professional advice.

Maybe Suicide Is Easier

Naturally, you expect us to convince you here that you should not commit suicide. But the truth is, our shouts of "No, don't do it" are not too enthusiastic. If you are going to commit suicide, you are going to commit suicide. You really don't have to, but if you want to opt for the angry, destructive way out, there is little anyone can do to stop you.

On the other hand, if you were serious about suicide you probably would have done it already. You would not have picked up this book and looked in these pages for some sort of support. You have already passed the point of total despair and destruction if you have come this far. So let's get on with living.

But if you are hurting so bad and feel so desperately alone that you are still thinking about taking your own life, you must approach those feelings as your first problem. The help you need goes beyond simply reading the advice in this book.

Look up "Suicide Prevention" in the Yellow Pages, and don't close the book without copying down the phone number. Or call the operator and ask for the number of the suicide prevention center in your area. That piece of paper with the phone number is your promise that someone is waiting to help you. In most areas, someone is available on the telephone hot line twenty-four hours a day.

Suicide is a rotten solution to any predicament, especially a predicament where someone is kicking you in the head. Better to be angry and fight back, depressed as you may feel.

Substituting alcohol for your lost love is just another form of suicide. Now is a good time to consciously cut back on your drinking, both social and solitary.

When you are at a party, switching to soft drinks sometime during the evening will enable you to think clearly and speak rationally. You can still enjoy yourself (if it's a good party) and you won't have to worry the next day about how much and what you said to whom.

Take a serious look at your drinking behavior when you are alone. If the after-dinner drinks run right into the nightcap, or if you need something stronger than coffee to face the new day, there's trouble. If you are thinking about alcohol while still at work or if you have been binge drinking periodically, it's time to call Alcoholics Anonymous. There's an active group in every community. You might not have known about them before because you never needed them. This organization has helped literally millions of people with drinking problems and their families. AA is listed in every phone book.

Suicide and alcoholism are emergencies that need the response of support organizations with trained, sensitive staff prepared to give you immediate help to see you through the crisis. They will direct you to other agencies; help is available if you need it. Remember, it never helps to solve one problem by creating another.

Where Does It Hurt?

Although your situation may not fall into the "life-threatening" category, the problems you are facing may still be serious. You need to think clearly and plan how you are going to take action to deal with your problems. For a start, poke around and find out where you are hurting; determine what needs attention first.

The previous chapters, which detail the emotions during each particular stage of emotional development after betrayal, give specific guidelines on how to cope with the feelings and problems of each stage. Here we are concerned with some of the more general areas that might need your attention.

If you have chronic physical ailments or are troubled by new symptoms, first schedule an appointment with your doctor for a medical checkup. Be sure to let your doctor know that you are under stress and ask for recommendations for a specific counselor and therapist if you need one. Marital trauma places great stress on your physical system, and stress can affect you in a myriad of ways. Second, check your body over carefully yourself. If your spouse is having or had an affair, he or she may have passed on to you the "gift" of a sexually transmitted disease. Don't just worry about symptoms; see a doctor. A conscientious doctor will want to help you with your emotional reactions to any physical problems you may have.

Maybe you are having trouble defining exactly what kind of help you need right now. Sometimes it is hard to specify one critical area; the experience after betrayal is often one of generalized hurt and confusion. You may be over the initial shock, but you want to feel better about yourself and to do something about coping with your pain and getting on with your life.

Perhaps you are already receiving professional counseling but also feel the need for a safe social situation, a comfortable peer group to see you through the hard times. You could call the contact person of a support organization, one that you feel might suit your particular needs and interests. Often these contacts are trained counselors or group leaders, either professional or volunteer, or else they are persons selected by the group because they are sympathetic listeners and qualified to share information about their organization. They may be persons who have recently made adjustments in their own personal lives similar to your own. If they have already "been there," they know firsthand your fears and apprehension; they will help you, even in that initial phone call.

The rejection by or philandering of your spouse may have left you with bruises beyond your broken heart—like damage to the area of your wallet, checkbook, or credit cards. If this is the case, a call for help to your banker or lawyer is in order. Even though you may still have tears in your eyes, don't overlook your need for financial and legal advice.

How to Find the Help You Need

After you've zeroed in on the type or types of help you need, your next step is to investigate your options. Find out exactly what assistance is available to help you handle your specific problems.

A lot of your research can be done today, at home or on your lunch hour at work. Start by checking the Yellow Pages or the consumer telephone directory under the headings "Human Services" and "Social Services." Here you will find listings for a wide variety of agencies and organizations. Make a list of those that interest you.

A phone call to your public library will put you in touch with a reference librarian and a wealth of free information. Almost every public library maintains a current, comprehensive file of community and social service organizations, complete with agency profiles and descriptions of services, fees, locations, and contact procedures. One client told us that a librarian was able to refer him to a men's support group which held weekly meetings in the library's community room. While you are talking to the librarian, ask for recommended books, magazines, and pamphlets that would be helpful for you. Don't be shy. Library information is free for the asking, and you might meet some new friends during the search.

Another rewarding phone call could be to the secretary of your local church or synagogue. If you call during office hours and explain your situation, the secretary should be willing to give you the names and phone numbers of church-affiliated groups and other organizations used for referrals by their pastor or rabbi. Don't worry about being a member; churches and synagogues are to mirror the love and care of God to all people.

While you are using the phone, call the local community colleges and universities. Ask for "Continuing Education" and request information on noncredit programs. Glancing through the catalogue of a university in the Washington, D.C., area, one can find "Coping," "Handling Your Emotions," "Reentry," "Displaced Homemakers," "Living Through Divorce," to list but a few of the courses. Many schools also have special counseling departments that could be helpful. The community mental health units at nearby hospitals may also offer courses that could be helpful in your situation. All of these services are considerably cheaper than a professional therapist.

Newspapers frequently run a listing of "Events for Singles," usually as part of the weekend section or with a syndicated column of special interest to singles. This will give you a wide assortment of organizations, from divorced/singles church clubs and parenting groups to little theater associations and bowling leagues. These groups usually list upcoming activities, regular meeting dates and locations, and a phone number to call for further information. If your local newspaper does not carry this type of feature, check the papers of the largest nearest city. A group there could help you locate a branch that meets in your particular area. The result is bound to be worth the price of a long-distance phone call.

A personal recommendation is one of the best sources for discovering not only what is available but what might be worthwhile. This is especially true for finding reputable counselors, therapists, and lawyers. A satisfied client is usually willing to give a glowing recommendation; likewise, an unhappy one is eager to complain and save someone else the aggravation he or she has had to endure. Joan came to us for counseling on the recommendation of a coworker at the bank:

"I knew that Alice took a shorter lunch every Thursday so that she could leave early for an appointment, but I'd always thought it was a regular tennis date. I was surprised when I overheard her tell someone she was going to a therapist. Alice seemed so squared away after her divorce. I never guessed she was getting help through counseling. When I got up the courage to ask her about it later, she was really helpful. She seemed to know just what questions and worries I had: How much does it cost? What do you talk about? What if you cry, or if you don't feel like talking? Alice didn't go into detail about her personal problems, and I didn't pry. But she gave me the informaion and encouragement I needed."

Counseling or therapy is not just to solve a crisis. Many therapists concentrate on growth and adjustment. Even if you feel you have the situation under control, you might still benefit from psychotherapy.

Once you start looking for support organizations, you may be very surprised to find out just how many of these groups and agencies exist in your area and the variety of interests they cover. Communities are recognizing their need to provide more than just schools, sewers, and police protection for their residents and are looking to help with other areas, including emotional problems. Networking, the nonprofit sharing of talents through support groups, is spreading rapidly throughout the country.

If nothing else, the plethora of self-help groups points out that you are not left dangling in the wind. Your problems may be unique, but there are many others with similar experiences.

You would be making a sorry mistake to ignore the practical advice and emotional support that are available to you from community groups and agencies. In the past, you may have shunned the Scouts, ignored fraternities and sororities, and rejected the Rotary and Welcome Wagon. For whatever reason—disinterest, fear, business commitments—some people simply avoid joining organized or even casual groups and keep their wallets happily uncluttered by membership cards. That attitude can change rapidly when you truly need outside support.

"Misery loves company!" you say? No, it goes deeper than that: men and women are learning that they share human needs and they can offer support to each other, especially in times of emotional suffering. Look upon these groups as communities of persons much like yourself— struggling, in pain, growing, desiring support and friendship.

Choosing Your Support System

Among the many support agencies and organizations, some are available any time of the night or day to help with urgent problems. We've already mentioned suicide-prevention centers and Alcoholics Anonymous. In addition, special twenty-four–hour hot lines are prepared to handle other crises, such as drug abuse, child abuse, and battered spouses.

What about counselors and therapists? How can you tell who is good and who's not? Should you use someone in private practice or should you go to a less expensive public clinic or mental health center? If you've decided to speak with a private counselor or therapist (here the terms are used interchangeably), it's most important that you feel comfortable with the person you have chosen to help you with your problems. Your time and money are going to be spent, and you want to spend both wisely.

While they may have received similar education and professional training, all counselors are certainly not created equal. They vary in their approach to treatment, in costs, and, of course, in personality. The best way to find out who is best for you is to ask questions. If you know people who are receiving counseling, ask if they would tell you a little about their counselors. Don't cause embarrassment by prying into their reasons for seeing counselors. Let them know you are looking for firsthand recommendations and that you value their opinions.

What should you be looking for in a therapist? If you are paying for private professional services, you want a qualified mental health professional. Psychiatrists, psychologists, social workers, and therapists should be certified by their particular national or local professional organizations, such as the American Psychological Association (APA) or the

American Association of Marriage and Family Therapists (AAMFT). Professional organizational credentials should indicate that the member has had appropriate education and licensing, and that he or she participates in peer review and continuing education. Don't be afraid to ask for credentials and references. You may have to interview two or three therapists before you find who's best for your needs.

When you make your first appointment, ask about fees. Some therapists charge for the initial consultation. Be certain you understand exactly what the charges are and check your health insurance, if you want to use it, to determine whether therapy is covered and the amount which will be reimbursed for out-patient counseling services.

Most therapists conduct sessions for forty-five or fifty minutes. At your first meeting, ask about the counselor's availability after office hours. Is there a hot line for emergencies? If you had a Sunday evening crisis, would the counselor be accessible? Is there a charge for phone consultations?

In the end, you alone can decide if you feel at ease with a particular therapist. A personality clash could interfere with your counseling progress. One client told us she had spent two months going to a therapist who was overweight, balding, wore a bow tie, and let his glasses slide down his nose. "He reminded me of an uncle we'd always made fun of when I was a kid. I just couldn't concentrate during our sessions and I could not work up any confidence in him, probably because he looked like goofy Uncle Andy. I decided to find someone else."

The same criteria would apply if you decide to use the counseling facilities of a public mental health agency. These counselors should also be trained in mental health treatment and be licensed by the state. Since public health agencies are supported by funding, their services are available on a sliding-fee scale. Ask that the fee structure be explained to you.

Public mental health agencies frequently offer a wide range of services and will be able to refer you to their special problems groups. If, as a parent, you think that your children would also benefit from counseling at this time, the agency could probably help with that as well.

Again, even in the clinic situation, you should be comfortable and confident with your counselor. If you have significant personality differences or feel uneasy, discuss it with the director of the agency. Although the cost at a mental health center is usually less than you'd pay for private counseling or on a sliding scale, you are still entitled to courteous and professional treatment. However, you may not receive the same type of personal and individualized treatment you might receive from a private therapist.

Talking with a Member of the Clergy

If you are an active member of a church or synagogue, perhaps you would feel comfortable seeing a member of the clergy for support at this time. Some of them have been trained in counseling and mental health treatment, others have not. It's perfectly acceptable for you to ask about their credentials and training in mental health and pastoral counseling.

Make it clear that you need counseling and advice. This is not to devalue spiritual guidance but to underline the importance of being specific in explaining your needs to the priest, rabbi, or minister. You are not looking for sermons or pious sayings, but for solid advice and someone who will listen. Some of the clergy are excellent counselors and the designation of "pastoral counselor" can indicate professional competence.

On the other hand, being a member of the clergy does not automatically mean that one is a competent therapist or counselor. Therapy is a specialized field requiring specialized training and experience. The training to be a leader of a religious community does not, as a rule, include specialized training to be a therapist. Some clergy receive this training, but most do not.

Most of the clergy are prepared to give you temporary emergency help. At those times when you feel you have no place to turn and you need a sympathetic ear, the accessibility and concern of a trusted member of the clergy can be comforting and inspiring.

The clergy may refer you to a church-affiliated social service agency such as Jewish Family Services, Catholic Charities, or Lutheran Children's Aid and Family Services. These and other religious-affiliated organizations can be excellent resources for many problem situations. As their names indicate, they are geared to helping families in stress. If you have a religious background, you may feel most comfortable seeking a support system based on your spiritual beliefs.

Support Groups—Helping One Another

As we walked into the basement meeting room of the church, we were surprised at how many brave people had come out on this cold, snowy December evening. Three or four people were filling in "HELLO, my name is————" tags at a table by the door. "First names only," said the smiling man with the marking pen. There were five or six men and women lined up near the coffee urn, waiting to fill their Styrofoam cups. A young woman opened the cellophane wrapper on a box of cookies to add them to the tray on the table, apologizing, "Sorry, these aren't homemade."

Another dozen or so people were already seated on folding chairs. A few chatted with each other. Some sat alone, concentrating on drinking their coffee. Their ages ranged from late twenties to early sixties.

We were quickly greeted and ushered to seats in the front of the room. Within a few minutes everyone settled down with coffee, cookies, and name tags, and the monthly meeting of the East Shore Community Support Group was underway.

After newcomers were welcomed, announcements were made of upcoming events: weekly small-group meetings, a holiday dinner at a restaurant, a sledding party for members with kids, and a request for volunteers to help get the organization's next newsletter in the mail.

We were introduced and began our discussion of "Picking Up the Pieces." As we talked, some heads nodded in understanding and agreement at certain points. A few in the group dabbed at moist eyes. Some stared and seemed frozen in boredom or maybe anger.

Discussion began immediately. Personal stories were shared, some with tears, a few others with nervous laughter. Almost everyone had something to say; some spoke of anger, others of rebirth. Friendships were being made. At ten o'clock the custodian knocked on the door and said he wanted to lock up. "Besides, you people are going to be snowed in if you stick around any later." Several people cheered that announcement.

As the meeting broke up, a small group was formed to continue the discussion at a local bar. As we brushed the snow off our windshield, a man came up to the car. He was one who had not spoken a word all night; he had seemed bored in the room. "I just wanted to thank you. You'll never know how glad I am that I came to the meeting tonight," he said in a husky voice. Then he was gone.

Something must have been said that night that helped him. Some words spoke to his experience, some sharing with the others. It did not matter who said the words or even what was said. It was important that he drove home that night knowing that he was not alone with his problems.

If you looked in the phone directory, called the library, checked with community or church organizations, or searched the newspaper for support groups and organizations, you probably found more than you'd ever imagined exist. Before you jump into a group, check to determine whether they have a specific purpose, what the age range of the members is, and whether trained leaders are present.

An organization such as Parents Without Partners can help you even if you do not have custody of your children. This is a solid, well-organized program with chapters across the country. You are sure to find one nearby. PWP offers self-help, educational, and social activities. They have a good reputation and are worth exploring.

Church-affiliated divorced and separated singles groups vary their focus according to the membership of each group. Some involve their clergy in programming, while others just use the church facilities as a meeting place.

Other specialized groups exist to meet particular needs, such as overeating, drug abuse, how to handle anger, reentering the job market, and so on. You will find a group to meet just about any problem you can think up or fall into, and there are even some groups dedicated just to having fun. Choose what you need.

Most organizations do charge a nominal membership fee; some just ask for a donation at each meeting to cover the cost of refreshments. Unless a social service agency or church is funding the group, someone has to cover operating costs.

In trying to decide which group is best for your needs, you might speak with one of the members or read a few issues of the newsletter or schedule of events. Question the contact person for the group. This person should be well-prepared to tell you whatever you want to know about his or her organization. But the very best way of determining the worth of a group is to attend a meeting.

If it appears that this group is not for you, do not feel obligated to go any further just because someone spent time on the phone with you or because you attended an initial meeting. Why waste your time with a group that is concerned with single-parenting problems if you do not have children or if they have their meetings at five o'clock downtown and you work until six in the suburbs? You cannot join a group whose activity schedule lists ski trips and New York theater tours if you are thinking about applying for food stamps.

When you find an organization or group that seems on target for your needs, give it a try. Write their next meeting date on your calendar in red ink and promise yourself to make whatever arrangements you have to in order to get to the meeting. Most people experience a certain amount of fear when going to the first meeting. Others are just as afraid as you. Many groups have a "buddy system" for newcomers. If you need a ride or just want someone with whom you can go, they will probably help you out.

First-meeting jitters are natural. You may feel awkward, but so does everyone else at first. Remember that the members of the group want to welcome you and help you feel at ease. That is what support is all about. But if you feel that you are still not wanted after giving it a fair shot, then head for the door.

Think about how you will introduce yourself. There is plenty to say about yourself besides, "Hi, my name is Judy and my husband is screwing around with his dental hygienist and I've never felt more rotten in my whole life," even though that is what you would really like to shout out. Save it for later.

What you can expect from most groups is support, not a magical cure—someone to listen, to let you cry, or at least shout if you don't cry in public, to share experiences, and maybe even to make suggestions. You must learn to cope with your own problems. A support group will help by offering encouragement, friendship, and some advice while you're making your own decisions.

As all of this happens, you may form friendships with some of the people you meet in the group. However, don't be dismayed if a few years from now you do not recall their names. The situation is similar to a group of people waiting at the airport for a delayed flight. Everyone shares the aggravation and tension. Soon, travel stories are told and help is given. "Here, let me hold your baby while you get a cup of coffee." You are stuck, and together you make the best of it. As soon as the plane arrives, everybody returns to their individual lives, and the group dissolves. You no longer need each other's support, but being together made life a little easier at that moment in time.

On the other hand, you may possibly find close friends in a support group, friends who will see you through your most trying moments and remain friends for many years.

As a member of a support organization, you might not always be aware when someone else is benefiting from what you are saying or how well you are listening to his or her story. Nonetheless, you will probably find yourself helping others with their problems. Sometimes helping another is the best antidote against self-pity. Going and helping is better than sitting home alone listening to old records.

Life 101—Learning to Cope

The adult or continuing education departments of most colleges and universities usually schedule self-help seminars and courses in addition to their academic offerings. You can sign up for an all-day assertiveness training seminar or a six-week course on coping with mid-life crisis, or with divorce, or with finding a job. Some schools have programs designed specifically to help women who find themselves alone and thrust into the work force.

Campus courses can give you self-help guidance and personal growth skills as well as provide a supportive atmosphere. The fees for these noncredit programs are usually quite reasonable. Some schools have funding for those unable to pay.

The community recreation department or local YMCA/YWCA often schedule similar self-help courses. Check the qualifications of the instructor and ask about the format of the course. This type of program is not advisable if you need serious professional counseling, but it might be ideal if you are looking for a broad approach to problem-solving in a low-key support group.

While you are investigating the programs at the recreation department, check out the athletic activities. This could be the perfect time for you to join an aerobics dance class or the community softball team, or to swim a few solo laps in the pool. Exercise is especially important if you are feeling depressed. A regularly scheduled regimen followed religiously can be of great help.

Other adult education courses—gourmet cooking, craft instruction, language refreshers, book discussion, drawing and painting—can be pleasant diversions. They won't directly help with your problems, but they will help you think about something else for at least a few hours a week.

Religious Support

There is a bumper sticker that says "When all else fails, try God." Spiritual support really should not be a last-ditch resource. If you have an active religious belief you probably turned to your faith after the first crushing blow of betrayal. If you have trusted in God for support during life's other trials, this will probably be the first place you turn.

On the other hand, you may have been raised with a religious faith, but as time passed you let your religious practice slide. This crisis may have led you to respond to a forgotten God. Faith can be a great solace and comfort and provide a rock in the middle of what feels like a swirling river.

You may be very angry with God right now for "letting" this happen to you. As a child, maybe you prayed for your sick grandmother. It did not make sense to you when she died. "If I prayed to God, why didn't He do what I asked? Did I pray hard enough? Is He angry at me? Is He punishing me for something I did?" You could be reliving the same feelings of abandonment now, only they feel even worse. It is easy to transfer some of the feelings of betrayal to God. For you, He may take on a share of the blame for allowing this to happen.

A hospital chaplain who does extensive counseling with cancer patients told us that he allows his patients to express their anger at God. "It's an honest reaction, and it's better to admit your feelings and face them head on. It's okay to be mad. Actually, He's probably rather used to those reactions."

A marvelous little book was written several years ago in response to the crisis of faith in a deeply religious man when his son, Aaron, was taken from him by the disease progeria. Progeria is a cruel disease which prematurely ages children, turning them into old people while they are still children and killing them when they are teens. Harold Kushner and his wife learned that their bright and lovable son had this disease the day his wife delivered their second child. *When Bad Things Happen to Good People* can inspire even the nonreligious person. It tries to make sense of seemingly meaningless and destructive tragedies which occur in our lives.

Faith can blur when you experience the crisis you are now enduring. But this may also be the time you are called to mature and develop an adult faith. "God writes straight with crooked lines," someone once said while reflecting on the pain in life. Isaiah put similar words into the mouth of God when he wrote, "For my thoughts are not your thoughts, nor are your ways my ways" (Isaiah 55:8).

Many churches have small prayer groups which meet, usually every week, simply to pray, to share life's happenings, to celebrate and give thanks for the happiness in the group members' lives and to ask for help in their difficult moments. Most are informally organized and meet in members' homes. Some get together for breakfast before work, while others meet over lunch at work.

Like all support groups, these vary according to the needs and interests of individual members. Many prayer groups include Bible study. Some are charismatic and have a unique spirit-filled approach to prayer; others concentrate on healing not just physical ailments, but also emotional and spiritual wounds. Some groups sponsor inspirational speakers; others focus on quiet prayer or reflection.

If you feel comfortable with this type of spiritual support and are open to shared prayer or meditation, one of these groups could be the answer to your prayers, or at least help you formulate the prayer. Inquire at the local church or synagogue or ask friends. Follow the same procedures in choosing a group as we discussed earlier in this chapter.

In Conclusion

The sooner you ask for help, the sooner you will find yourself moving forward, taking charge of your life. In summary:

1. Ask yourself what you need. Professional counseling? Legal advice? A support group?
2. Find out who can help you.
3. The hardest step: call for help.
4. Follow through. If one support system does not work out, try another.
5. Give yourself credit for taking charge. You're doing something constructive to cope with your problem and get on with your life.

11

What About the Children?

Should your children be involved in the emotional process that takes place when your spouse requests a separation or when you discover that he or she is having an affair? No!

Will they be involved? Yes! You can't stop it. However, knowing that they cannot be kept out of the process, you can better decide on the best way to handle their involvement. That is what this chapter is about.

Children often become involved at the very beginning, when they are apt to overhear the heated arguments between their parents, the accusations and threats. They love both parents, so for them there is no winner. Sometimes parents actively drag their children into the conflict, trying to win them over to one side or the other. Sometimes children hear about affairs from other relatives or friends rather than from their own parents.

If children are not enmeshed in the conflict during the initial stage of shock, they are brought into the problem if and when their parents begin to think about and discuss separation. At this point the practical reality must then be faced: "Where will the children go if we can't save our marriage?" Also, because the growing emotions of anger and depression normally affect the betrayed spouse so deeply, those around him or her are bound to be affected, especially the children.

In one way or another, then, children are dragged into the ugly mess. They can be hurt very badly in the short term, and the emotional scars may very well last the rest of their lives. As a parent in this situation, your task is to minimize the amount of damage that is done to your children. In general, the more you can maintain your composure and the less you tear down your spouse in front of the children, the less you will draw your children into your anger and depression and the better off they will be. Unfortunately, however, you may become so caught up in your own emotional trauma that you will tend to forget that the children can hear most of what goes on and understand more than you can possibly imagine.

Children are like sponges when it comes to their parents' emotions. They seem to absorb the tension and act it out in their own childish ways. Some children will begin to have nightmares, while others will have night terrors wherein they wake up screaming, trembling, and perspiring. Some will begin or resume a pattern of bed-wetting.

Most children will begin to react negatively to both parents and also to their brothers and sisters. They will become rebellious, talk back, and throw temper tantrums. Often they will fight with their siblings and sometimes with other children in the neighborhood.

Teachers may call home and report that your child does not seem to be concentrating and won't accept correction or discipline as he or she did in the past. If a teacher calls you in for a conference, tell him or her that there is trouble at home and that your child's change in behavior could be related to your domestic problems. Request that the teacher keep this information confidential. If a separation is imminent, insist that the teacher make no mention of it to the child until you have had an opportunity to discuss the matter with your child yourself. Once the teacher understands the situation and sees the probable cause of your child's behavior, he or she will be much more patient and understanding and may help smooth this difficult period of the child's life.

Taking a Positive Approach

If you think your children are aware that there is a problem between you and your spouse, it is best that you briefly and unemotionally discuss it with them as soon as possible. Children are apt to feel cheated and offended later on if their parents do not at the outset tell them that there are serious problems. Above all, don't refuse to discuss the matter with your children if they ask, and don't send them away.

If your problems cannot be worked out, and if, having gone through the decision stage, you have opted to leave your spouse (or if your spouse has left you), sit down with your children and calmly inform them that things are not going well between the two of you and that you will probably be living separately. Keep the discussion simple; do not go into details or argue your own case. Tell your children that you and your spouse feel it will be much better for the whole family if you separate. If your children have overheard arguments about an affair, honestly explain that your spouse would like to be with someone else. No more need be said.

Affirm that your child is loved and that he or she will be taken care of. Children need to be assured of this fact repeatedly because the very foundation of their security, the family, has been shaken and broken. They need a reinforced sense of stability, to know that even though a rift has occurred they will not be abandoned.

Try to keep your composure in front of your children. You may have some "special places" away from them where you can cry, yell, rant, and rave. These might be a friend's home, therapist's office, or an isolated room where your children cannot hear you.

Sometimes you may not be able to control your grief or rage. If you kick a chair or cry uncontrollably, tell your child frankly that you are feeling bad, but that you will get through the hard times and sad feelings. Also reaffirm that he or she is still loved and that this has nothing to do with him or her.

Children are flexible and resilient. If you can maintain your dignity and control, your child will probably weather the storm quite well.

Do Not Confront Your Spouse in Front of the Children

Children seem to have little antennae which are attuned to marital conflict. We would probably be astounded if we could look into a child's spirit and see how deeply hurt he or she is when parents angrily scream and shout at one another. Think twice before you confront your spouse within earshot of your child. Just because it is dark does not mean that the sound in your house is blotted out. If anything, sound travels better at night, because there is little background noise to interfere with angry voices. If you are in the kitchen or the dining room fighting or just discussing an affair or separation, your children can very well be listening to that conversation.

Some people confront their spouses in front of their children with such angry words as, "See what your father is doing?" or "How can you do this to me and the children?" They may be trying to gather the children for support, especially if they feel alone and beleaguered, or they may be attempting to punish the other parent. Either way, it will be at the expense of the children.

Just as harmful for your children would be any attempt to win them over to your side in your spouse's absence. Don't involve them in sordid details, and don't confide secrets to them and then swear them to silence with such words as "But don't tell your mother." This type of secret will place a horrible burden on your children, who will feel torn in two different directions, not wanting to betray either parent. Consider how difficult it is for us adults when our friends are experiencing marital conflict and we feel that we are asked to take sides with one or the other. How then can we expect a defenseless child to take sides between parents?

Do not tear down your spouse in front of your children either by describing infidelities or by pointing out his or her character flaws. Your children will have to maintain their relationships with both of you. The more positively children can relate to both mother and father and the more children respect each of them, the healthier will be their adjustment and maturation. As difficult as it may be, try to remember this principle when discussing your spouse with your children. Tearing down your spouse probably will not really hurt your mate but it almost certainly will hurt your children. Only in the most dire circumstances, when you are honestly fearful for the welfare and safety of your children, should you take action to remove them from your spouse's influence.

Beware of Venting Your Anger on Your Children

It is natural at this time to wish occasionally that you had never had children. They seem to be in the way, always underfoot, and a complication. They demand a great deal of attention at a time when you need a chance to be alone and think. You may feel that the last thing you need now is whiny children wanting this or that.

Francine described the guilt these feelings gave her. "I wish someone had told me after I found out about Alan's affair that these feelings about my kids were okay and that I wasn't evil because I was impatient and angry with them. I often got angry at the children, sometimes even hitting them when they did not deserve to be hit. Then I would feel so guilty. I felt I was going to pieces and that I was taking out my anger and frustration on the kids."

"I remember one night when I burned the supper," said Phil. "Ellen had just recently left, and I couldn't cook worth a damn. I was so tired and angry, and the kids were whining and complaining and fighting with one another. I took the casserole, still smoking away, and dumped it upside down in the middle of the kitchen floor. I screamed at the children and told them if they wanted to eat, they could eat off the floor. Then I told them to go someplace else.

"At that point I caught myself. Their mother had just left and I knew that they felt rejected by her. I couldn't reject them too, although at that moment I wished they were with their mother and that she had the work and problem, not me."

Feelings of anger toward your children are natural and to be expected as you go through the emotional stages of reacting to betrayal. There is nothing wrong with having these feelings, but you must learn to handle them.

It is easy to displace your anger on your children. Like a man who is abused at work by his superior, at whom he cannot strike back, and comes home and beats his wife and children, the betrayed person has no place to vent anger but at those closest and least defended, the children.

Be aware of the tendency to displace anger. Take great care at this time not to hit or slap your children. It is better not to discipline your children now with physical punishment than to risk overreacting and use your children as convenient objects on which to vent your anger. Be especially patient with them at this time. They too are under a great deal of stress.

Prepare Your Children for Your Separation

As we've said, your children should be told *before* a separation takes place and one of you moves out of the house. If possible, however, avoid discussing the separation too far in advance, as the children will worry and try to influence their parent to stay.

Children most often blame themselves for the separation of their parents. They usually think that they have done something to break up the marriage. They are often flooded with guilt and remorse and need ongoing reassurance that the blame is not theirs, that they did not cause the separation.

If possible, both parents together should tell the children what is going to happen. Plan in advance what you are going to say. Explain to the children that both of you will still be there for them and that both of you love them. Explain who will care for them on a day-to-day basis and how visitation will be arranged.

Tell the children they will be able to go and see the home or apartment where the parent who leaves will stay. It is important for them to feel they have access to the departing parent, and they should be encouraged to visit that parent early in the separation period.

When discussing the separation with your children, try to stay under control. Children will be less confused and more secure if they feel that their parents are acting rationally and have control over the situation.

Don't Burden Your Children with Your Own Problems

Your children are very vulnerable at this particular time. Don't try to rely on them for support in your time of need. Look for other sources of support, and discuss your problem with friends, relatives, and professionals.

Some parents, feeling rejected and abandoned, will cling desperately to their children for support, thus involving them in battles with their spouses. We have even heard horror stories of parents who have taken their children along to spy on their unfaithful spouses. What a tremendous burden this places on the child who loves both parents and does not want to see either of them hurt!

One woman, bitter about her husband and determined to show her daughters what a louse he was, told us the following story:

"It was his birthday and he had to be out of the country on business. I'm sure he took *her* along. I told the girls that we were going to celebrate Daddy's birthday while he was gone.

"I baked a big birthday cake and decorated it with forty candles. Inside I put a giant firecracker with a long wick. I took the cake out in the backyard and we all sang 'Happy Birthday.' Then I lit the long wick and we ran back to the house.

"Boom! The giant firecracker went off and blew the cake to smithereens."

Don't give your children a burden with which they will have to struggle for the rest of their lives.

This advice also holds true for adult offspring. Sons and daughters who are in their twenties, thirties, and forties still feel that the relationship between their parents is sacred and inviolable, even if they themselves have gone through a divorce, or experienced infidelities in their own marriages. It is far better for everyone concerned if you and your spouse handle your own problems.

12

Putting Humpty Back Together Again . . . Maybe Better This Time

If you have opted for trying to reestablish a loving and committed relationship with your spouse, you may already realize that you have chosen what, in many ways, is the most difficult option open to you. There are, you'll find, no easy answers. You have been through a terrible trial, and it will take a long time to overcome the agony. But it is possible to start over. Even though your relationship can never be put together the way it was before the betrayal, you can still, possibly, build a new trusting relationship.

Joan struggled within herself for many months before she made her decision about Hal:

"I remember very clearly the moment it came together for me. I was furious at him and I had to let the hate spill out first. I remember when I started screaming. It was something like, 'Get away from me! I hate you! You're a slimy skunk.'

"A pillow I'd ripped off the bed to throw at him knocked over a lamp. We both froze at the sound of glass and seashells smashing to bits on our bedroom's parquet floor. Between us lay the shattered fragments of the lamp we'd bought on our honeymoon on Sanibel Island. It was a clear glass ginger jar filled with shells we had collected along the beach. My shrieks of anger turned to sobbing.

"Earlier that night, Hal had tried to initiate a 'let's kiss and make up' scene, but I was in no mood for reconciliation. I hadn't been for months—but he kept trying.

" 'Joan, honey, stop crying. We'll get a new lamp.' He put his arms around me.

"We'd had sex after I learned about the affair, but only for a short while. Lately, every time he touched me I'd flinch and pull away. This time I let him hold me. 'I don't want a new one, I want the *old* one,' I whimpered into his shoulder.

"Looking at the shards of glass and pieces of shells I knew it was impossible. So was the old marriage. I think he realized it then, too.

"As I swept up the mess, I discovered a few shells that had somehow survived the crash. I set them carefully on the dresser. Hal plugged in the lamp cord and the unexpected brightness startled us both. The shade had probably protected the bulb from breaking.

"We stared at each other, seeing something in the shadows cast by the single bulb. The old lamp was smashed, but the light was still on. And there were enough important pieces left for us to try to put together a new one.

"That night we decided to try to do the same thing with the pieces of our marriage. We started to talk seriously."

If you told friends and relatives about your partner's betrayal you probably heard the advice, "Dump him!" or "Are you crazy, you're still living with her?" or "Spoiled fruit, throw it away." After all, almost one out of two marriages ends up in the divorce court for one reason or another, and surely an affair is sufficient grounds. On the other hand, maybe you take your investment in the marriage more seriously than some of the others who rush to court.

Is divorce the best answer for you?

Your answer to that question is as personal and complex as you, your spouse, and the circumstances of the betrayal. Only you can give the answer. An affair is certainly a serious betrayal, but, as crushing as it may be, it is not, in itself, a reason to end a marriage.

As we have seen, there are different types of affairs, ranging from a brief fling to long-term commitment to someone your spouse avows to love. Your initial reaction to the betrayal may be the same in either case, but clearly your hopes of salvaging your relationship are more realistic if your partner protests he or she still loves you and has left the other person for good.

Is your spouse or lover suffering deep pangs of remorse, bringing you presents, asking to go for counseling, or do you sense that he or she is breathing a sigh of relief and is waiting for you to give permission for a fast exit? If your partner honestly affirms that he or she does not want to leave you, you might wonder if down deep he or she wanted you to find out about the affair. Maybe your discovery wasn't so accidental. Was your spouse trying to say in a cowardly way, "My bags are packed, I want out," or was it rather a plaintive cry of, "Can't you see? I want better; it's not good enough, what we have now. Maybe something this serious will make you see that we are drowning"? Not an easy question, but if you take your marriage seriously, and if you want to attempt a reconciliaton, you had better answer it as honestly as you can.

Trying to rebuild a marriage can be a lot harder and take a lot longer than sending in the demolition crew and calling it quits. Separation and divorce are not easy, but at least the end result is certain. There is no guarantee that you'll live happily ever after if you decide to forgive and rebuild.

All the energy you have been expending on anger, frustration, and conflict will have to be redirected to forgiveness, renewing commitment, and caring. (The word "loving" may not be a word you are ready to use yet.) No magic potions can be stirred into the coffee every morning to bring about a healing. We hate to use the word "work" when it comes to a relationship, especially what should be a love relationship, but the truth is, rebuilding a love relationship is hard work.

Starting over means change. The two of you will have to abandon the habitual patterns that gave you security. Such changes are frightening and difficult. Right now you may feel that about the only thing you want to cooperate on with your spouse is writing his or her obituary, but cooperate you must.

There is no guaranteed formula for success, but once you have made the decision that you would like to give rebuilding a try, the following questions, as well as the questions posed in chapter 8, might help you clear away some of the mental and emotional debris.

1. Do you care for your spouse? Do you care enough to forgive? Would you just as well get rid of your partner, saying "Good riddance to bad rubbish"?

2. Does your spouse care for you? Have you asked? Do you believe the answer?

3. How have you handled your feelings through each of the four stages after the betrayal? Do you feel capable of making decisions about your future? In other words, have you reached the fifth stage?

4. Are you both willing to spend the time and concentration on revitalizing your relationship?

5. Can you speak frankly with your spouse about such matters as money, sex, fidelity, children?

6. Can you listen to him or her without being defensive and expressing anger?

7. Would you be willing to see a marriage counselor for professional help to rebuild your relationship?

You may have zipped through all the questions without a single "yes" answer but still want to stick with your spouse because of the children, or for reasons of financial security or social convenience. Many people decide to remain together for reasons such as these and eventually they work out an accommodation with their spouses.

Maybe you've decided to stay put just to give yourself time to sort matters out. If this is the case, then the relationship will only be bandaged, rather than healed. Eventually, the basic problems between you and your spouse will arise again and worsen. Without direct action for drastic change you may get the time you need, but you won't find happiness.

If you feel you are ready and willing to work on your commitment to your partner, to hang in and rebuild your relationship, and if he or she feels the same, then Humpty Dumpty may have a chance for survival. Time to find the superglue and hunt for the missing pieces.

There Are No Rules in a Knife Fight

When someone pulls a knife on you, you throw away the rules and fight for your life. If, after slashing away at one another, you and your spouse decide to rebuild your relationship, you'll have to set aside the deadly weapons and abide by the rules.

What are some of the deadly weapons that have to be buried? Sharp words that cut and gouge and will not be forgotten. Caustic comments and harsh accusations are weapons of destruction. Your anger and frustration may justify your throwing a few daggers, but eventually the effect of constant verbal punishment will be deadly. As your feelings of anger, resentment, and hurt rise to the surface, you might notice your voice rise and your finger point. These too will have to be set aside. If you are serious about working out your relationship, you'll have to overcome your urge to punish and get revenge for all the pain you have felt.

Once you have both laid down your weapons, certain rules will have to be imposed.

Forgive, even though you can't forget.   You may have heard from others that you will have to forgive and forget if your relationship is to succeed. Don't believe that for a minute. You *will* have to forgive to the extent you can, but you will never forget. Some scars will always be there, but you have to make a firm resolution not to bring them out and use them as weapons in battle. Forgiving is essential, however. You might have to bite your lip until it bleeds, but you cannot punish your spouse indefinitely if you want to rebuild a new relationship.

Joan told us about how she kept punishing and punishing Hal. They were trying to work out their relationship, but Hal could no longer stand Joan's constant nagging punishment and he stormed out of the house. Joan, who had consummate tact in her executive position at work, just could not keep her mouth shut at home.

"I did not want to keep badgering and punishing him, but I could not stop myself. I was mad enough to kill him. Finally everything collapsed one night when I screamed at him that he'd never cared about me but sure paid plenty of attention to her. He flew into a rage and stomped out. It was winter and he forgot his coat. Realizing it was really cold, he spun around on the front steps and pulled the door handle so hard he tore it right off. He asked for a divorce after that. I really had tried to forgive him for the affair, but it all came back whenever we were under stress or when an argument started."

Without forgiveness, you'll never be able to start over. Trying to rebuild without forgiving would be like trying to work a jigsaw puzzle with mittens on your hands. Forgiveness does not mean capitulation, however. On the contrary. You can and must set down your minimum requirements. Lay down your rules, and see if your spouse can agree and abide.

Trust one another.   Someone you once trusted has violated your trust. The natural tendency is to say what one salty lady told her husband during a joint counseling session: "Up yours. Once you've been screwed, you keep your legs together. All I got from trusting you was venereal disease."

Rebuilding damaged trust takes time and testing. During that time you may find your suspicions sneaking up on you: you may still wonder about every strange phone call, out-of-town meeting, and dinner-party flirtation. You'll have to learn to handle such suspicions. If you shadow your spouse's every move and try to overhear every conversation, you won't be able to regain trust. Trust must be earned. Your partner has to have the freedom to prove to you that he or she can act freely and yet maintain a commitment to you. He or she has to have the liberty to prove to you that your trust is deserved.

For many persons trying to reconstruct a relationship after a betrayal, regaining trust is the most important and the most difficult step. It is the glue that binds any serious commitment.

Be faithful.   You probably feel that sexual faithfulness is absolutely essential for success in rebuilding your relationship. If so, make this one of your absolute, minimum requirements.

But what is required of your partner must also hold for you. A get-even affair will sabotage your future. Work toward finding the lovers you need in each other.

Put rebuilding your relationship at the top of your priority list.   Your relationship deteriorated for one or several of many reasons: poor communication, demands of a job, family concerns, alcohol, financial worries. Whatever the reasons, those reasons were probably given priority over maintaining a nurturing relationship with your spouse. The order of priorities in your life has to change.

Obviously, you can't be expected to quit your job, send the children away, and ignore relatives, friends, and other important aspects of your life. But your relationship must be more important than anything else. Time and effort must first go into your relationship—and *then* into the other aspects of your life. If you don't organize your priorities in this way you may as well kiss your spouse good-bye right now.

Set realistic goals.   Clarify what end result you seek. What's your bottom line? If you're trying to recapture newlywed bliss or your early carefree days and nights of romantic banter and sexual discovery, you are going to be disappointed. Not that your sex life can't be exciting or that romance is gone forever, but what you shared together in the past can't be used as a standard for measuring your new relationship. You have both changed and your relationship will be different. In some ways your relationship may be more enriching than before, but "carefree" and "blissful" are not descriptive of a partnership that has been shattered by betrayal. A new "unwritten contract" has to be formulated, and together you will have to discover fresh expectations for your relationship.

Be willing to accept change.   You both have to change, even though it was your spouse who was having an affair. You will have to be more spontaneous, less critical and abrasive. You will find yourselves talking to and listening to one another more than ever. Affection will grow and you will begin doing little caring acts for one another—watching for one another's needs.

Sex will gradually become more meaningful, and intercourse will become a loving act. It will be less inhibited, and you will hold and kiss each other more frequently.

You can't become someone you are not, but the positive, caring aspects of the real you will blossom in the sun of a caring relationship. Unlike the pleading stage, when you may have tried to be the perfect spouse for your partner in order to win him or her back, you now act in a concerned way because you genuinely care about your spouse.

Que sera, sera.   Rebuilding a relationship takes a considerable amount of time. Good lovers will tell you that the process continues indefinitely and that they never take their partners for granted.

The milestones marking your progress will be very difficult to perceive. You can't compare your rebuilt relationship to your previous one or to the way your friends down the block get along with one another. It will be a new creation.

Learn to communicate.   You and your spouse may at first have a difficult time sitting down and hearing each other's story and figuring out how the two of you are going to change in order to get your relationship back on track. Reading this book together may be of help. A good counselor or psychotherapist will also be of assistance. But these are only crutches to facilitate the key process. Ultimately, the communication process—and the success or failure of your marriage—is up to the two of you. That process can be summed up in three phrases. Embroider them in gold needlepoint and hang them over your bed, chisel them in the concrete over your front door.

Talk to each other.

Listen to each other.

Understand each other's feelings.

Communication

The most important skill in all human relations is effective communication. All humans communicate, that is, all send and receive messages about ideas and feelings. Only a few do it well.

Today communication is taught and counseled. Debates are held about it, and communication theory is developed. Communication forums are cropping up in business and social organizations all over the country. Despite all this, few people pay real attention to *how* they communicate unless a serious problem is caused by their lack of communication. Amazingly enough, most couples live their lives together without discussing their likes and dislikes, sex life, feelings, needs, and fantasies.

If you want to build an intimate relationship with someone, you must learn the skill of intimate communication. This skill embraces not only talking and listening well but also the art of making sexual love well. Both are forms of communication of equal importance.

In our experience, the key to effective communication lies in the following three steps:

1. Use "I" language. Speak assertively about your feelings and needs, using the word "I" as the subject of your sentences. "I feel this is right" and "I want you to do this or that when we make love" are much more effective than "You are wrong" and "You don't make love correctly." Statements using "I" language do not force the other to feel judged. "You" statements are finger-

      pointers which cause the other to set up barriers from behind which he or she fights or withdraws.

2. Reflect back what the other person says. "Here is what I understand you to be saying" or "You feel hurt when I speak about this" are examples of effective reflections. When you listen, try to understand your spouse's emotions, not just the words said. Then reflect back those feelings and words. This will help you to truly understand without being judgmental. If you can show empathy for your spouse, he or she will be much more open to your feelings and opinions.

3. Negotiate and compromise so that each of you can obtain what he or she feels is important. Compromise demands both flexibility and caring. It is the opposite of blind capitulation—when you cave in and then become angry and depressed. Compromise demands that you give, but at the same time you will get what is really important to you.

Although these three steps may sound simple, in reality they can be very difficult to implement. Still, if you can master these steps you are well on the road to a fulfilling, nurturing relationship. Developing the skill of communication is worth all the time you can spare, and a counselor who can help you improve communication skills is worth any price.

Here are some helpful hints to aid you in sharpening your communication skills, especially in the context of improving an intimate relationship:

- Trust and honesty are imperative, but be careful that you are not being honest just to relieve yourself of guilt. For example, there is very little use in revealing an affair you or your spouse has had. Such revelations will only hurt your relationship.
- Don't retreat into silence when the going gets tough. Problems are not solved by silence. Anger and frustration build and eventually ignite an explosion or are buried in depression. Don't expect your spouse to understand you when you don't speak. You may be trying to make passionate advances with your sexy eye movements, but your spouse might be thinking that your contacts are bothering you. Say what you mean and ask for what you want.

- Nagging, dredging up the past, and going over the same issues again and again interferes with true communication. Sarcasm and insults are variations on this same theme, as is steamrolling—trying to overcome your spouse's opposition by shouting it down.
- Any past affairs must be buried and placed off-limits. You can't change the past. Probing for details, making snide remarks, or persistently reminding your spouse how deeply you have been hurt will only continue to drive a wedge between you. You may need to ventilate your feelings about your spouse's affair, but you should have taken care of that in the final stages of your emotional reaction to betrayal. To continue on after that time is not productive. If you still need to talk about the pain of betrayal, see a therapist; don't air your emotions with your spouse at this point.
- Listen to yourself. Are you following the three key steps? You may be surprised at what you hear.
- Laugh. Humor makes for good communication and brings a feeling of well-being to the person who laughs. Sex, too, can be greatly enriched by play and laughter. Therapies have been developed using humor as the main ingredient, and medical professionals have reported that laughter causes a beneficial chemical change in the human system and can actually cure certain physical ailments.

As you begin your new pattern of communication you may find, as do many couples who rebuild almost lost relationships, that there is a lot you do not know about your spouse. Successful communication patterns do not mature overnight, however. They take time and concentration.

Two very busy people *can* find pockets of time to share, no matter how busy their schedule. Try cutting short a phone call when your spouse walks in the door or saving the newspaper to read on the train and chatting over breakfast instead. Make a quick phone call to your spouse during lunch or between appointments. Move the television out of your bedroom.

For some couples, dinnertime is the best opportunity to touch base. One of the most ugly weapons defeating communication is the television. What an abomination to have one in the room where people eat! If you want to converse and learn about another person you cannot do it where a television is droning away.

If you have a family, dinnertime is a time to be shared, not just in gulping down the meal, but in letting everyone have a chance to talk about their day. Sometimes, however, a couple should have meals without the children present, so that they can focus on one another.

Some couples go out for breakfast once a week; others take a walk together in the evening instead of watching the news. If bedtime is one of the few times you have together, use it to catch up on the day's events, but don't use this time to bring up problems. Most of us are too tired to try to solve problems then. Anger mounts easily and the desire for lovemaking is dampened.

You might read in some of the more popular magazines about cute gimmicks like looking at each other's schedule books and making an appointment to see each other. If you find it necessary to resort to the appointment method, you'd better check to see if rebuilding your relationship is really the number one priority in your life.

Once you find the time to talk with each other, what are you going to talk about? Everything! The weather, inflation, the children, the dog, your Aunt Tillie's will, Woody Allen movies, you name it. Once you develop a rhythm (good communication is like good lovemaking), you can venture into important matters like your sex life or how you should spend your money. You can't just sit down cold and communicate about topics closest to your hearts. There is a natural progression in the depth of dialogue; give it time.

Think back to when you were dating. You tried to know everything about the other person; no detail was too trivial to be discussed in endless conversations. You may no longer be starry-eyed, but you and your partner must still have some refreshing and fascinating words to say to each other. "Hi . . ." is always a good start.

Sharing daydreams is another way to improve your communication. Pick a quiet, relaxed moment—while lying on your backs watching the clouds, perhaps, or lying in bed after afternoon lovemaking. Daydreams are intimate, and we're not apt to reveal our secret thoughts and feelings unless we trust the listener. "What would you do with a million dollars?" "Where would you like to go for an extended vacation?" "Where do you hope we'll be in ten or twenty years?" How would you answer these questions? Do you know how your spouse would answer them?

If you find your conversations are one-sided, you might try an exercise we use when working with commuter couples who are separated for extended periods of time. One person talks about any topic at all for fifteen minutes, while the other person listens and shows interest but does not respond verbally. Then the first person remains silent while the other person talks. After both have spoken, a dialogue can begin. You will be surprised at how difficult this exercise is at first. You will also be surprised at how much more understanding you both acquire about each other's feelings and life.

Timing is another important factor. Bringing up a major sexual conflict as he's running off to catch the bus or expecting a romantic response while she's telling you about an argument she had at work is hardly reasonable. Common sense and ordinary courtesy are used so readily with strangers and often forgotten with the people we love.

Children can sometimes be a real stumbling block to a couple's efforts at dialogue. The routine chaos of family life can absorb all of a couple's time and energy if they do not plan ahead for themselves. Since there is a great deal of anxiety involved in rebuilding a marriage, your children can provide a convenient excuse for you to avoid one another and concentrate on their needs. Be aware of this tendency, and keep your priorities straight.

Plan "together time" for you and your spouse. At least one evening a week should be reserved for adults only. Put a lock on your bedroom door, if one is not already there. Take a walk or ride without the children several times a week, if that is possible. An occasional weekend in a motel without the children can do wonders for communication. Above all, always try to go to bed at the same time.

Conflict is natural in any communication, unless you are Ozzie and Harriet. Expect the conflicts and learn how to negotiate compromises. Watch for trigger points—those topics which cause pain and anger in your spouse. Triggers are pulled only in order to punish. They serve no constructive purpose and should be avoided.

One trigger for most couples is money. For instance, a wife who knows that her husband is very sensitive about not making as much money as his brother might pull a trigger and say, "Jack seems to make enough money, why don't you take some lessons from him?" Or a husband might gripe to his homemaker wife, "I work like a slave and you spend it like water." Anger is often displaced onto the money issue, and many couples struggle for power through a struggle about money. In-laws are often another trigger: "My parents told me never to marry you," or "Why can't you learn to get along with my family—it's the least you can do after what you've done." Frequency of sex and disciplining the children are also common triggers.

Couples trying to rebuild their relationship must learn where the trigger points lie, and then both have to agree on how to handle these issues when they arise. If you cannot develop an approach to the trigger points, you will have a most difficult time trying to rebuild an already limping relationship.

After identifying the trigger points, you both need to agree on a method of breaking into the destructive communication pattern. This may entail one of you calling to mind previous discussions about trigger points and that each of you agreed to make an effort to cool off and change the subject. In these crucial moments remember to use "I" language. Always speak about your feelings and needs and do not use "you" language, which attacks your partner and makes him or her defensive.

If you can identify and neutralize the trigger points in your relationship you will develop more effective communication patterns. Your relationship will improve dramatically. But the process of developing more effective communication is not easy. You will find that both of you, on occasion, will slip into the old patterns. Slowly and patiently, however, if you are conscious of your slips, you will gradually be able to build better communication patterns and, consequently, a better relationship with your spouse.

Sex After Betrayal

You would not be trying to pick up the pieces of a shattered relationship if you discovered that your spouse found a new bridge partner or made a new friend at work. You might feel jealous, but not betrayed. You feel betrayed because your intimate bond of trust and reliance was broken, the bond that was symbolized and lived out through your sexual commitment to each other.

You would be unusual if you did not now find it difficult to work out a new sexual life-style. After you discovered your spouse's affair, your sex life may have surged briefly to new heights. As we explained earlier, this is common in the pleading stage. But then a deep anger probably began to envelop you and you felt cheated and rejected. As your anger grew, your desire for sex decreased. Now you may very well find sexual activity with your spouse repulsive.

"The feelings got so strong," said Francine about Alan, "that I would get up from bed and want to vomit after we had sex. When we were in the middle of intercourse I would picture them making love together, wondering what they had done, where and how she touched him. Did he feel her breasts, take off her clothes? I tried to push the thoughts out of my mind but they kept creeping back.

"I really tried to love him, but I just could not relax. He knew it, too. We would lie there after intercourse, saying nothing. God, did I feel confused."

After their wives have had affairs many men have difficulty getting and keeping an erection. A deep gnawing anger, often unconscious, prevents them from giving through sex. Sometimes they are able to perform, but once they begin to worry about their performance, regular impotence can set in. Repeated episodes indicate the need for a good therapist.

Women may develop a lack of sexual desire after the discovery of their spouse's affairs or find that they are unable to have an orgasm. Some women may also find intercourse painful, a condition called dyspareunia.

On the other hand, some people whose spouses have had an affair are sexually turned on. As one client told us: "I would never admit it to her, but I used to get excited thinking that some other guy wanted her. She seemed sexier after the affair. Somebody else wanted what she had to offer. I hated him for it, but I enjoyed her a lot more afterwards."

For most of the people we interviewed it was years before they could honestly say that they did not think of the affair while having sex with their spouses. There is a natural temptation to question new sexual techniques your partner may want to explore with you. Phil told us that he had to squelch saying, "Oh, and just who taught you that?" "Somehow," he said, "just having sex with Ellen would unleash peevish, angry feelings and I would think things like that, even though I knew she was trying with all her heart."

The truth of the matter is, hard as it may be for you to face, your partner may feel sexier, more desirable, more erotic because he or she has had a new sexual experience with a lover. Remember, though, in the long run this new self-image may be to your benefit as you reap the enjoyment of a sexier partner. Every cloud has·a silver lining.

Rebuilding Your Sexual Relationship

If betrayal has made a wreckage of your sex life, it is possible to rebuild it. The very best way to go about rebuilding is creatively to change your sexual patterns, to give your lovemaking new life.

First, talk with your spouse about your sexual needs and interests, because if you don't converse about sex, your sex patterns will probably not change. Problems in a sexual relationship are frequently related to communication difficulties that appear in other areas of your life as well. Why leave the success of your sexual relationship to chance or allow it to stagnate while you work on other areas of your relationship?

"Our sex life is boring," is a common complaint. Phil's wife, Ellen, told us: "Sex with Phil was like following the same route to Astabula every Friday night. First the left breast, then the right, then the hand between the crotch. How many times do you take the same route to Astabula before it becomes boring?"

Sex often becomes boring because couples are too anxious or embarrassed to try anything new. Yet monotonous sex can readily become a sensual adventure if partners are willing to tell each other what they want: more tenderness, more cuddling, more aggressiveness, new positions, more experimentation, new settings for lovemaking—whatever.

Sex is a shared creative experience in which you use your body to please the other person and yourself. Your spouse cannot please you unless you indicate what you want, what makes you excited, how you turn on. Begin to express some of your fantasies. If you don't have sexual fantasies, try to create some. Watch some erotic movies or read some erotic books and let your imagination run.

There are dozens of sex manuals suggesting new techniques. No need to be embarrassed about buying these today, or asking for them at the library—they are usually best sellers.

Listen to what others have to say about their sex lives on radio talk shows and television shows. Many people call in to our show and tell us that they listen to us with their spouses. Hearing others talk about sex openly and frankly may reduce your anxiety and give you ideas about how to renew your sex life.

Popular magazines carry many articles related to sex, covering—or rather, uncovering—everything from "Putting Spice in Your Sex" to "10 Ways to Achieve Orgasm." If you would prefer to have help tailored to your situation, you can contact a sex counselor or sex therapist. The

American Association of Sex Educators, Counselors and Therapists in Washington, D.C., will provide you with a listing of sex specialists in your area.

Don't be put off by suggestions that seem bizarre to you. Sexual appetite is personal. There is no standard, normal, usual, or general way to enjoy and communicate through sex. Not every sexual encounter is a two-hour orgy with whipped cream and strawberries (when was the last time you tried *that*?), but not every sexual encounter has to be a two-minute ho-hum fulfillment of an obligation, either.

An important element in sexual communication is nonverbal, out-of-bed sexual language. Sharpen your skills of flirting, touching, hugging, and nibbling; learn how to use erotic eye contact and choose sexy clothes. Some couples take mini-vacations, if only to the local Marriott or Holiday Inn. Others use their creative imagination, leaving erotic notes in books or under pillows, getting an X-rated movie for the VCR, wearing sexy new underwear (this holds for men as well as for women).

Underlying all of these approaches is a change of routine. If you are reluctant to change, talk to your partner about why. If you are too fearful to talk to your partner about sex, then it is definitely time to get some outside help.

Ideally, in rebuilding a relationship, you would like to rely on a rock-hard foundation of forgiveness, trust, sensitivity, nurturing, communication, and a dynamic sex life. No one has all of these all the time. No relationship, not even the very best, is perfect. It is not fair to have unrealistic expectations of your partner. He or she will occasionally make mistakes, be insensitive, be a lousy sex partner, and fail to communicate.

However, if you are going to rebuild a relationship, you can at least expect your spouse's continuing effort. If you cannot get that much, throw in the towel and head back to the lawyer. You may as well start over with someone else. At least you have given the relationship your best try.

There is no guarantee that Humpty Dumpty will ever fit back together again, no matter how desperately you try. However, if your relationship thrives, and well it might, you could fall in love again with a person you once loved and the two of you can once more enjoy a nurturing and fulfilling life together.

13

Choosing to Leave—
The Single-Life Option

After having been married for some years, no matter how unhappily, people considering the single life-style are apt to paint a picture of going home to an empty and silent house, eating a solitary meal of canned beans, and climbing into a large, cold bed to spend a restless night tossing and turning or staring into the darkness with tears rolling down their cheeks.

This sad picture can be a real possibility. But, before you accept this as your way of life, reflect on two points:

First, remember your feelings as your marriage began to drown. Nothing is quite so lonely as being in the same house and in the same bed with someone who's neglected you, betrayed your trust, and who may not be in love with you anymore. Recall your feelings of frustration and anger, the depression, and sometimes hatred you felt.

Second, you can paint yourself a different picture of the single life. You can go home to a house you have decorated the way *you* would like. You can eat cold beans if you want to when you are too tired to cook, and no one will criticize you. You can stay up as late as you like, watch television in the bedroom, munch potato chips in bed. When you

163

want to go to sleep, you can go to sleep. If you want to go out with someone new and exciting, you may, and you may return home whenever you want.

You can do all of this and much more and no one will belittle you, criticize you, or make you feel guilty. You will be free to give and nurture as well as to take and enjoy yourself. You will also be free to find a committed and loving person.

People can be miserable whether they're married or single. Some persons see the single life only as a transition stage before passing once again into the married state. Others embrace the single life-style as a way of life and genuinely enjoy being single. Marital status does not determine happiness. What determines happiness is the way you handle yourself. This chapter will explore how you can build for yourself a rich and fulfilling single life.

You Are Not Alone

Whether you have made the decision to get divorced or that decision has been made for you, you are not alone. In 1983 more than 2.4 million couples were married and 1.18 million couples were divorced. As the divorce ratio soars upward it appears that in the not-too-distant future just as many divorces will occur in a given year as marriages. The number of marriages in 1983 was 60 percent of what it was in the year 1960, while the number of divorces climbed 200 percent over that same twenty-three-year period.

From 1950 to the present the number of people living alone has increased by nearly 400 percent, from 4 to 19 million, and more than a third of those living alone are under 45 years of age. As of March 1978, more than one U.S. household in five consisted of someone living alone. Single-parent families increased more than 70 percent during the past decade, while two-parent families decreased 4 percent. In short, the single person and the one-parent family are no longer the anomalies in our country. The unmarried life-style, with or without children, has become part of mainstream America.

Fears about Living Alone

Being single can be an exciting challenge, and a chance to change and grow. Why be afraid or skeptical at this juncture in your life? If you do feel frightened, you may be harboring some of the common misconceptions about single living. See if the following ring a bell:

I cannot manage on my own.

I will have to be sexually promiscuous if I date.

People won't want to be with me if I am not part of a couple.

No one will want to marry me again.

I'm not capable of attracting and holding a mate.

I'll never trust another person intimately again.

I'll be so lonely that I'll want to die.

I'll never be happy again; I'll always feel depressed.

Most people who move from marriage to the single state feel some of these fears about themselves and about their future. If you are used to having a spouse who makes decisions for you, goes everywhere with you, and with whom you have commingled most aspects of your life for years, the prospect of living alone and independently may be harrowing.

Besides the fear within that you might feel, there are certain obstacles from without. Our society traditionally has considered the married state as the "normal" life-style, although that idea is changing. From family fares on airlines to father-son and mother-daughter dinners at school to company-sponsored business trips for employees and spouses, society creates obstacles for divorced persons striving for acceptability. Even some of your married friends may not be supportive of you at this time because they're too threatened by your change in life-style.

Even more daunting than the fears within and the obstacles from without, however, may be a basic doubt that drags many new single persons down like a pair of cement shoes. This is the ghost which raises its ugly head when you feel rejected: "I'm not lovable, I'm not adequate, I am not *good* enough."

Just because one person has rejected you for someone else does not mean that no one on earth will find you desirable. And the fact that your spouse wants a divorce from you does not mean that you will not marry again or that you will not be able to stay married if you do. Most divorced people remarry, but some find the single life so liberating and challenging that they will choose not to marry again, at least for a while.

Some of your friends will stand by you, and there will be many new friendships to enjoy. If some of your former friends and acquaintances are uneasy around you because you are no longer part of a couple, then you will move on and choose others as friends who value you just because of who you are.

You will find that some of your friends and relatives are prejudiced by stereotypes of single people. Some of these stereotypes may be lingering in your own mind, too. Forewarned is forearmed!

The swinging single. The most common stereotype is that all singles are sexual sybarites or deprived nymphomaniacs and constantly jump into bed with one and all. Sex to them is as casual as saying "hi." Most of them have herpes, but you can never be sure, because no singles tell the truth about venereal disease—or birth control. Given half a chance, a single woman will trap you by getting pregnant.

The single parent. Pity the children of single parents! Divorced parents are unreliable and irresponsible. Their children are left unattended; go to bed whenever they want; live on potato chips, hot dogs, and Twinkies; never eat fruit or vegetables; and only have a hot meal at their grandparents'. They are bound to become delinquents—or worse.

As for the noncustodial parent—what more need be said? Noncustodial means noncaring. The children will be fortunate to see their noncustodial parent once or twice a month, and then usually for an hour (less, if it's a fast McDonald's). When they pick up the children, they're invariably late—without so much as a phone call, apology, or excuse.

The divorced man. He thinks he can have any woman he wants. Hordes of single women pursue him constantly, and he is usually exhausted from the many nights he spends in riotous orgies. He keeps a sailboat for entertaining bikini-clad 20-year-olds and a penthouse in the city for steamy afternoons. He may be looking for a steady relationship—but not for marriage. He just wants someone to do the cooking, shopping, cleaning, and laundry.

The divorced woman. A sad case. She could not hang on to her man, because she just couldn't satisfy him. Now she's desperate, panting after anything in pants, doing anything to hook a man: inviting him for dinner, doing his laundry, spreading her legs—anything. She is to be pitied. You can fix her up on a date with anyone. "Any man is better than no man," she says.

She is also to be feared. She's on the prowl, obviously, and anyone else's man is fair game. Watch your husband because anyone can be seduced by someone *that* needy.

Yes, there are some singles who fit these stereotypes, but the vast majority of divorced men and women are responsible parents, live ethical lives, and are capable of nurturing relationships.

From where do the stereotypes arise? Most probably they have their foundation in the antiquated notions that divorce implies a moral weakness and a fatal flaw in the divorced person. In any event, these stereotypes persist and must be dealt with.

Beware of stereotypical thinking. It can ruin your self-esteem and feed your fears. Root it out of your mind and be prepared to meet it in others.

Time and the successes you find will prove to you that all of these obstacles to leading a fulfilling life as a single person are surmountable. By calling on your inner strength you can abandon your old securities and find new joys.

What's Good about Living Single?

Your first step into the single life must be to find out who you are. Possibly you have submerged your identity for some time in your marital relationship. If so, you are now in a position to re-create yourself. As the great philosopher-theologian Paul Tillich wrote: "Man is what he makes of himself. And the courage to be as oneself is the courage to make of oneself what one wants to be."

This creative process is not as ponderous as it may sound at first. It involves setting goals, testing and experimenting, seeking new knowledge and skills. You will make choices and through these choices find fulfillment and enjoyment.

Learning to enjoy life is fundamental. When you are happy within yourself you will find yourself enjoying others. You will seek out new directions, new friends and experiences. What's more, since you are no longer part of a couple, people will now react and relate to *you*.

For Gerald, this was a wonderful discovery: "I always thought that I was quiet and never had anything interesting to say. No one would want to be alone with me—they'd die of boredom. I always relied on Marina at social gatherings. She did all the talking and joking and carried every party. When she left and our old friends started to invite me out by myself (though not all of them did), I was flabbergasted. In fact, I even said to one of my friends, 'Why do you want to be with me? I'm such a dud when it comes to social life.'

"Can you believe that I let my self-esteem sink so low? I wouldn't wish what happened to me on anyone, but Marina really did me a favor when she left. For the first time in years, I feel that people want to be with *me*, that they enjoy my company. I never knew that when I was with Marina, because she talked for both of us.

"You want to know something else? Someone told me that most of our friends thought Marina was a bore. That Bozo she's running around with deserves her. Let her talk for *him* now."

Being single will also give you the freedom to date and to form new sexual relationships. Most probably intimacy either died in your previous relationship or was fading fast. Discovering new possibilities for loving intimately is one of life's finest pleasures, and it now lies ahead of you.

There will be many other freedoms for you to enjoy. For instance, you may have given up dancing while you were married, because your spouse hated it. Now you can dance as much as you want without having to coax an unwilling partner. You can take those skiing lessons your spouse thought cost too much. Unless you have children, you are free to come and go as you please.

Don't bury yourself in responsiblities. There is a tendency for the person entering the single life to use the dedication to work or the care of children as a defense against leaving the protective walls of a home. Take time to exercise some of these freedoms and enjoy your new life.

Above all, think and act positively. If you take charge of your life, you can create a wonderful new world for yourself and turn the negatives mentioned at the beginning of this chapter into pluses.

I cannot manage on my own.	I can take care of myself just fine, thank you!
I will have to be sexually promiscuous if I date.	I will have the opportunity to enjoy and develop sexually as I decide.
People won't want to be with me if I am not part of a couple.	I will have many new friends, some single, some married.
No one will want to marry me again.	I will marry when I am ready.
I'm not capable of attracting and holding a mate.	I am lovable in my own way.

I'll never trust another person intimately again.	I will trust someone who trusts me.
I will be so lonely that I'll want to die.	I'll have the time to do what I want to do.
I'll never be happy again; I'll always feel depressed.	I'll find happiness as I begin to take charge of my life.

Happiness Is Taking Charge

Taking charge of your life as a single person involves three steps. The first step is adjusting to the single state, the second involves gathering resources for life as a single, and the third is moving out into the community. In the life of a single person all three steps can take place simultaneously with the focus shifting periodically from one to another.

Settling In

Moving from the married to the single state of life will take adjustments and modifications on your part. First, you will need time to heal and improve yourself, since what you have been through recently has no doubt drained you physically and emotionally. Much energy goes into coping with the emotions of the five stages. Take some time now to relax—pamper yourself a little.

Among the first adjustments you will need to make are getting used to sleeping alone and eating properly.

Eat well.   Initially you will probably find your eating irregular and bothersome. Mealtime may also intensify feelings of loneliness, because you are probably used to eating with someone. Remember the following:

- Don't skip meals. Nutrition affects your mental attitudes.
- Plan your meals ahead. Planning will prevent the last-minute junk-food grab.
- Shop for fresh foods such as vegetables, fruits, cheeses, and meats at least once a week.
- Buy a "cooking-for-one" cookbook if you live alone. Inquiries at the local bookstore should turn up at least several possibilities.

- Don't use eating as an escape from loneliness. Eating can be soothing and assuring, and can therefore be overdone. You hardly need a lot of extra pounds as you enter the single world.
- When possible, invite someone to eat with you. Preparing food for others can make you feel positive and helpful.

Get a good night's rest.   You may also find that your sleep patterns are changing. Difficulty in sleeping is natural, but there are some things you can do to sleep better:

- Don't eat big meals late at night. Eat early and allow the food time to digest.
- Don't exercise vigorously late at night. Heavy activity stimulates your nervous system and keeps you awake.
- Drink warm milk at bedtime—the amino acids in the milk will act as a tranquilizer. A little liqueur added to the milk can improve the taste and increase your drowsiness.
- Keep a pad and pencil by your bed to write down any burning thoughts that are keeping you awake.
- Keep your bedroom well ventilated. Fresh linens have a soothing effect, too.
- Read a boring book or article at bedtime. This works better than a sleeping pill.
- If, despite your efforts, sleeplessness persists, consult your physician. He or she may prescribe a mild sleep-inducing medication. Of course, this is a time to be cautious when using sleep medication. You are under unusual stress, and medication easily can become an addictive crutch. Use sleeping pills only temporarily and under a physician's direction.

Start a program of exercise.   Getting regular exercise at this time will not only make your body feel more alive, but will clear your mind and improve your attitude. There is evidence to indicate that regular exercise stimulates the production of certain chemicals by the brain which induce a feeling of well-being. Exercise also gets you outdoors or into another environment such as a gym, tennis court, or swimming pool and gives you an opportunity to meet new people.

Create a pleasant environment.   Surrounding yourself with living things can also help. You may have children in the house and certainly they are evidence of life, but we also suggest that you have plants and flowers in your home. If you are struggling with loneliness, a pet may provide some of the companionship you crave. If you are remaining in the same house or apartment you've been living in, you might want to consider some redecorating or at least putting up some new pictures which you have chosen yourself.

Plan ahead.   Watch for times which are emotionally loaded—such as holidays, weekends, anniversary periods. With proper foresight, you will be able to spend these particular times with family and friends, instead of sitting in front of the television with a frozen turkey dinner for celebration. You can also plan on a daily basis, using the night before to write down what you are going to do the following day so that you will not be left with long open stretches of time in which to brood over your plight.

Do something special for yourself.   Do some of the things you have always wanted to do. You may have to set up a special savings account to live out some of your fantasies, but it will be well worth the effort. You may have been meaning to go to the Caribbean for the last ten years. Or perhaps you've wanted to take a course in art appreciation or continue your education. Maybe you've always wanted a good leather jacket but have never had the time to look for one. Or perhaps you've wanted to sign up for season tickets at the playhouse or take flying lessons or join a swim club. Whatever it may be, now is the time to do it.

Always have a project under way.   Maybe the closets have not been cleaned or reorganized for years, or the downstairs bathroom has been looking dingy and needs new wallpaper. Your file system is a mess. Get started on some task you need to do. It can give you a sense of purpose and accomplishment. Organizing your external world can also help settle the turmoil within.

Have some daily physical activity.   We suggested above that a regular exercise program is essential, but you can go a step farther and add a physical ingredient to your everyday tasks. Whenever you are feeling lonely, afraid, or just plain bored, push yourself into some type of physical activity to change your mood. Work in the yard, walk to the store, clean the garage or basement, paint the hall. Physical activity can distract and absorb tension.

Keep a journal or diary.   Write your thoughts as you go through new experiences and feel new emotions. Keep meaningful quotes of friends and authors who influence you in some way. Give yourself advice. Collecting your ideas and feelings at this time will help you better understand what you are going through, and later on you can look back to see where you were at a different time. You will also be formulating your own philosophy of life.

Gathering Resources

Do your homework: discover what is in your community and what possibilities are open to you. Talk to others, make phone calls, read and research. Some single people constantly complain that there is nowhere to meet other singles, that "all the good ones are taken," that there is nothing to do, and that their community caters only to couples. Don't believe it. These people probably have not done their homework or have not had the courage to act on the possibilities there.

To gather resources you will have to seek the support and information of others. The hardest step is usually the first: asking. You'll find, though, that people are genuinely interested in helping, just as you would be. You have only to ask. Do not be ashamed to admit to yourself that you are frightened or that you're not sure what direction you should take. Actually, most of your best contacts will be made casually— someone who sits next to you at a wedding, someone you bump into in the store, a fellow member of the PTA.

Carefully read local newspapers and magazines. Check for singles clubs and events. Local colleges and universities as well as civic organizations provide various activities. There are so many single persons in today's world that most institutions are developing programs directly suited to their needs.

Chapter 10 of this book covered the topic of using community and religious resources for a more specific purpose, but it bears repeating that there are many support groups for divorced people. Talking over your concerns, fears, and experiences can help take a burden off your shoulders. There are also support groups for children of parents who are going through divorce. Your children may need support as much as you.

Moving Out in the Community

Having done your homework and gathered information about available resources, you are ready to (gulp) venture out on your own.

"When Marina left me," Gerald told us, "I went into hibernation and licked my wounds for almost a year—going to work, keeping up the house, not going out. When friends called and asked me to come over I usually had excuses: too busy, going to one of the kids' band concerts, not feeling well. I just wasn't ready to face the world as a single person. I had to have time to rest, put my thoughts in order, get things in order.

"I still can't believe it took me eleven months, because I am usually a man of action: I see what needs to be done and I do it. Guess it was a pretty big blow for me—being left for another man."

Most people who have gone through the shock of betrayal need a period of time to "get things in order" before they can jump into the single world "out there."

The initial contacts are the most difficult to establish. After you have set up a small network of friends and supporters, the circle will spread. Eventually you will have more to do than time available.

Making yourself approachable can ease the process of entering the community. Here are some hints:

- Be sincere when meeting people.
- Show enthusiasm for the moment. Be optimistic.
- Pace yourself. Slow down your speech and movements if you feel very nervous.
- Make direct eye contact—this helps establish intimacy and overcomes nervousness.
- Say "hello" or "hi" with energy. First impressions count.
- Look your best. It reflects your self-esteem.

The most important ingredient for making yourself approachable is the value you place on yourself. People move toward persons who have positive attitudes about themselves and about life.

You will probably find yourself making many excuses for not going out or for not joining a group where you may meet others. You may be saying to yourself, "I can never go to a singles group—they'll think I'm desperate," or "Singles groups are for losers." As a matter of fact, singles groups are simply for people who happen to share the reality of being single. These people understand what being single means. They will share your ideas and concerns and are looking to have fun. This might be exactly what you need.

Still, if you want to meet members of the opposite sex, there are other avenues besides singles groups. Getting involved in volunteer work, politics, or civic organizations, furthering your education, or joining special interest clubs or groups might be a better way for you.

Areas of Special Concern for Singles

While being single offers excitement, challenges, new friends, and a more independent approach to life, several areas of this life-style require special attention. Don't think of these areas—namely, money, children, dating, and sex—as major obstacles, however. They provide opportunities for growth and change.

Money

Very few persons become single without some change in their economic status. For some this will be a first exposure to personal financial management. We will not attempt to get at the specifics of your financial needs and concerns here, but we can give you some general guidelines to help you deal more effectively with money.

- Figure out your financial needs. What do you have available? How much do you need to live comfortably? Do you have extra assets? What do you plan to do with them?

- Learn the basics of money management if you do not already know them. See a financial manager or talk with a friend or relative experienced with finances. You might attend some classes on money management and investments or read books and articles on these subjects.

- Use a cash settlement wisely. Don't just spend it. It could provide your future financial security. Develop a plan for its use.

- Figure out the best way to save your money. Savings accounts may not be the answer, yet at the present time you do not want to risk too much of your capital on high-risk investments.

There is no need to panic about financial security. In reality, very few people are truly secure financially. Try not to spend compulsively or hoard unreasonably. Plan for the future, and take the time to learn what must be done. Worrying about money will not ease your financial difficulties; careful planning will.

Children

After your divorce, you may notice that you have a closer relationship with your children. While you and your spouse were separating, both of you were probably tense and preoccupied with your own problems. You may not have been available for your children as much as they needed you. After the dust has settled, therefore, you both can make an extra effort to give them your time and support. Fathers, especially, are apt to develop more closeness and warmth with children than they exhibited while they were married.

Single parents often experience guilt feelings because of their divorce. The normal tendency is to overcompensate and deprive yourself for the children. This will often lead to a subtle anger and frustration in the custodial parent, however, and should be guarded against.

To be an effective single parent, you need to take time for yourself without neglecting your children. Don't try to be both parents for your children, just do the best you can. Children are naturally resilient and can adapt to most situations quite well, including the single-parent family. And, of course, the family atmosphere will be warmer without the angry arguments and tension that was present when you and your spouse were together.

If you are a single parent with custody of your children, you might keep in mind the following guidelines:

- Try to have at least one meal a day together as a family.
- Have a special meal on the weekends.
- Observe rituals and celebrations such as holidays and birthdays.
- Try to anchor your children in the extended family of grandparents and aunts and uncles.
- Give special time to each child.
- Read to your children before they go to sleep and assure them of your love.

- Don't tell them horror stories about your ex-spouse.
- Keep in touch with teachers and look for signs of emotional problems which might need assistance.

If you are the noncustodial parent many of the principles mentioned above apply to you also. But note also:

- If there is more than one child, each child needs special individual attention however limited your time with them may be.
- Children need to be anchored in your family as well as in the family of the custodial parent.
- Try to establish a routine when the children are with you.
- Do things together at your home, such as cooking meals, reading, playing games. Children get tired of outside entertainment.
- Keep in touch with them by phone between visits. Set up a regular time when they know you will be speaking with them.

One last point needs to be mentioned concerning children of single parents. They will have a difficult time accepting new opposite-sex friends with whom you may become involved. For a long time they will hold on to the impossible dream that someday you and your ex-spouse will come back together and the family will be one happy family as it was in the past. Introducing someone new as a possible future spouse can clash with the child's fantasy of a reunited family and be very difficult to accept. Some children will act with jealousy and try in subtle ways to drive you and your new friend apart. Be aware that they do not do this out of meanness or hatred, but rather to protect their dream. Be patient, but, after a decent interval of time—say, between four and six months—be firm in not allowing your children to dictate your needs and choices.

Dating

Newly separated singles can fall into one of three traps when they venture back into the world of dating and sex.

The first trap is the fear of making a mistake. Those frightened by bad experiences in their past constantly look for signs that the new relationship will turn out like the old—and so the new relationship withers on the vine. For instance, when a new man leaves his clothes hanging on the side of the bed or draped over a chair, a woman might say, "See, he throws his clothes around. He has to be disorganized. This can never work." Or if he speaks of saving money, she might see him as cheap.

On the other hand, a man with a new girl friend who works outside the home may find that she never offers to make him a meal because she often eats out. "Never even has food in the refrigerator," he says. "How could she ever take care of me and the children? This relationship can never work."

The second dating trap is panic over being alone. Some single people are so lonely, or more accurately, so afraid of being left alone, that they will do anything just to keep the other person present. They therefore ignore flaws and serious problems. We'll take care of that later, they think.

He says, "I love Chinese food." She would rather eat stewed cockroaches than Chinese food, but she is so afraid that he might take offense that she replies, "I just love Chinese food, too." On Friday evening, as she chokes down her meal at the Chinese restaurant, he smiles at her and says, "This is wonderful. Let's come back for Chinese food again next Friday." Some singles, so desperate to have a warm body, cling and hold on for dear life—eventually frightening away any potential spouse who comes along.

The third trap is anxiety over getting too close. These singles, like singles who fear making mistakes, respond to deepening intimacy with anxiety. Unlike those who fall into the fear trap and destroy their relationships, these singles come just close enough to hold on to their new relationships, but never really become intimate with another person. They will go to bed with another and speak of love, but they avoid any projection into the future or fantasy about a possible life together. They feel they must walk in shallow water and never swim, lest they drown.

Meg had been through two marriages and gotten hurt both times, once by a husband who abused her physically and once by a husband who left her for his secretary. Now she dates often, but she will never let her boyfriends near her children or involve them in any family outings. Quite a few have tried to enter into her life when she seemed to beckon to them. But as they came closer she closed the door just enough to keep them out. Meanwhile, she spoke often to her girl friends about how she could never seem to meet the right man.

Those who do not go through the five emotional stages after the betrayal experience have a difficult time forming new intimate relationships. For them, dating usually becomes a trying and anxiety-riddled experience. The freedom to relate openly and in a trusting way is directly related to resolving the inner conflicts that arise from betrayal.

Some general guiding principles can be spelled out:

Try to judge each relationship on its own merits. If you are waiting for the perfect partner, Prince Charming or Princess Guinivere, you'll be disappointed.

It is unlikely that you will meet someone who agrees with you on everything; he or she is bound to hold some values and opinions different from those you espouse. Be assertive about what you want and about your values, but learn to negotiate and work toward compromises you can live with.

The key to dating and developing promising relationships is to create new experiences that will push the old memories into the background. No one will drop out of the sky or pop, genie-like, out of a bottle with a "Hi, I'm your date for tonight." You must make your own moves first to find out who's out here. You might be very pleasantly surprised.

Sex

"After I was single for about four months I decided to join a singles group," Gerald told us. "I had heard that the single's world wasn't quite what it was when I was a teen-ager, but I don't think I really believed what I heard.

"I decided to try out a singles group, and the very first meeting I attended, I sat next to a rather pretty lady, about my age, who told me she had three children. After the meeting I asked her if she would like to go for a drink. 'Why go out?' she said. 'Just come on over to my place. I have something there.'

"She lived in a nice suburban home, even had a half-blind dog who followed me around. It seems like we had just sat down in the front room when she reached over and undid my tie. Next thing I knew she had her hand between my legs and was unbuttoning my shirt. My God, I had just met her three hours earlier. I really didn't know what to do. At first I kept telling myself that I really shouldn't be doing this, that my divorce was not final.

"She smelled nice and, God, it had been a long time. She stood up and slid off her nylons and panties. What the hell, I told myself.

"We did it, right there on the couch. Thank goodness the dog was half-blind."

"That wasn't exactly my experience," said Francine, "But I found out real quick that you could have just about anything you wanted when you looked around.

"I jumped into quite a few one-night stands and some longer relationships. It seemed like I had to work something out of my system, that I had to prove to myself that I was still desirable, that someone wanted me." Her face reddened slightly and she dropped her eyes. "I suppose I just needed to be told more than once."

The sexual rules "out there" have changed. Many single people no longer see sex and marriage as necessarily belonging together. When you reenter the dating scene, you'll find there are fewer sanctions placed on your choices and behaviors nowadays.

There is a much greater availability of partners for sexual activity than in the past, and Francine's statement that "you can have just about anything you want" is close to the truth.

Most new singles move in one of two directions. The first is what some have called the "first-year crazies." These singles are out to have intercourse with everything that moves. If sex is an appetite, those who have the first-year crazies are starving and will voraciously gulp down every sexual morsel they can lay their hands on.

Other singles move in the opposite direction. They withdraw—even after they have gone through the fifth and final stage of emotional development after betrayal—and they stay away from sexual activity. Many of them identify sex with permanent commitment, and they avoid commitment like the plague.

You will be placed in a position, when you begin to date, of having to make decisions about your own sexual activity. No longer protected by your married state, you will have to decide for yourself what is right and wrong.

Don't let others push you into a decision. Do only what you feel comfortable doing. Examine your religious and moral beliefs and make your decisions accordingly. If you do not feel ready for sexual activity and someone is pushing you, walk the other way. You have to work through your own emotions first, passing through all five stages, until you feel you can make decisions clearly and without guilt.

Before the breakup of your marriage, your lovemaking probably became a negative experience, especially if your spouse told you that you were inadequate or that he or she no longer loved you. You can easily carry the hurt from your bad experiences over into new relationships. It will take some time and work before you feel trusting enough to give yourself to another.

A Few Cautions

Some traps do exist for the single person, and you may be more vulnerable right after leaving the cocoon of marriage. Here are some of the pitfalls you might look out for:

Beware of the meet-market.   Unscrupulous individuals and groups look to make a fast buck in the loneliness business. They promise happiness and companionship, but their promises usually have a hollow ring. Dating services, escort services, gigolos, and pimps are there to take your money. Many singles bars appear lively and attractive but offer very little. Most people who frequent them looking for someone to relieve their tedium and loneliness find only rejection and end up feeling more bitter than when they entered. If all you want and expect is a one-night stand, fine—you will probably find it. If you are looking for more than that, however, you will probably be disappointed.

One woman described the singles bar scene in her city this way:

"Singles bars? Yuk! I used to go to several singles bars before I moved to the East Coast. I lived in the East for three years and then returned to Cleveland. For old times' sake I returned to some of my old singles haunts. Do you know that the same people were still standing around at the same bars still looking for the same magical someone! I couldn't believe it. Nothing had changed. If I went back there today I would probably still find the same old drags in the same old places."

You would be better off spending your time looking for reputable nonprofit groups and organizations which may not have the glitter of a singles bar but can offer much more.

Beware of seeing marriage as the answer.   Many singles look to marriage as the way to escape loneliness. However, if they thought back to their not-so-wonderful marriages, they would remember that there can be a lot of loneliness in marriage, too.

Second marriages have a higher divorce rate than first marriages. Part of that higher rate must be attributed to the fact that many singles too quickly jump into a second marriage. Singles who enter second marriages before they are ready will often encounter problems worse than those they encountered in their previous marriages, because they have not gone through all of the emotional stages of withdrawal.

Beware of using sex to try to keep another person.   If a person will stay with you only because you are great in bed, you should ask yourself if this is a person you really want around. The growth of intimacy and commitment depends on much more than sex. Sex without emotional intimacy leads to anger and eventually leads you to push the other person away.

Beware of the hope trap.   This is also known as the "if only" syndrome:

> If only he would come back . . . .
> If only we had a chance to talk some more . . . .
> If only she would leave him . . . .
> If only we could spend some time together . . . .

The hope trap is an indicator that you have not really come to grips with your emotions and gone through the stages of separation. Some singles continue to live with the fantasy that their spouses will return and that everything will be like it was (which was quite terrible, actually). They will continue with this fantasy even after they have been repeatedly kicked in the teeth, after all dialogue has ended, after trust and commitment have flown out the door. If your company goes bankrupt, your stock becomes worthless, so you sell it or burn it. The same holds for a relationship that is over. If you can't work through the stages and can't let go of your spouse and the unwritten contract you once had, get help from a good therapist.

Beware of involvement with married persons.   Sexual relationships wherein one party is single and the other party is married work to the disadvantage of the single person. The married person always has the security of someone to whom he or she can return. The single one doesn't have that security—for him or her the affair can only be self-defeating.

Being involved with a married person, especially if your spouse was involved with a single person, might give you a feeling of revenge. But at what price? Very, very rarely do these lopsided relationships work out. If you become deeply involved with a married person, you will only have to pick the pieces of glass out of your feet when that very fragile relationship shatters.

In Conclusion

Look for love, but as the song says, don't "look in all the wrong places." The old myth about not getting involved on the rebound is more false than true. It may be much to your advantage to go out and date early after the end of your marriage, especially if you feel you have reached the decision stage of your emotional healing process. Do not just take what you can get, however. Pick someone you can truly love, and who can truly love you, before you start making commitments.

14

Love Me,
Love Me Not

You have been betrayed by someone you trusted, someone to whom you committed yourself, someone with whom love once flowered.

Love me, love me not. After the experience of betrayal you pluck off the petals of your relationship, one by one. Can love be restored? Or is it slipping away forever? Back and forth your emotions toss you through the five stages. Finally, the last petal is plucked.

In the fifth and final stage of emotional healing a point of decision is reached. Then life must go on. You must let go of your old relationship and either rebuild with your spouse or go in another direction.

Those who cannot let go of their old relationships are dragged down into the quicksand of anger and depression. If you never shake free of the mire and cannot make a choice for a new beginning, your life will turn into a succession of bitter and sullen days. If, however, you can see the betrayal as an opportunity for new discoveries and excitement, if you face your fear and insecurity and take charge of your life, then you can grow a new flower, perhaps one even more beautiful than the old one.

All of us experience betrayal sometime during our lives. For close to one-half of the population that betrayal is a shattering of the fundamental trust placed in another person, either through that other person's sexual affair or an unexpected request for a divorce.

Because talk about affairs is everywhere in our society—in the media, the supermarket, the bedroom—and because separation and divorce are fast becoming the norm rather than the exception, we are sometimes led to believe that the discovery of a spouse's affair or his or her unexpected request for a divorce should not be all that earth-shaking for the person betrayed.

Nothing could be farther from the truth. Betrayal violates a person at the deepest level of trust, security, and commitment. With the force of a wrecking ball it smashes into a person's psyche and destroys his or her self-esteem. If you have been betrayed at this fundamental level, and even if you feel that you no longer love the person who betrayed you, you will ache for a long time with an excruciating pain. It is an ache that will never completely leave you. At certain times, such as anniversaries, weddings, family ceremonies, and holidays, it will return, not with the intensity of the original discovery, but with some pain nonetheless.

No two betrayal experiences end in exactly the same way. You may share the pain of betrayal with many others, but your solution is uniquely your own.

Each of the seven betrayed persons we brought together for this book has taken a separate and unique path. Where are they now?

Joan, who had always been so cool and sophisticated, had great difficulty in repressing her anger. She physically attacked Hal's lover and vandalized her car. She and Hal tried to stay together at first, but eventually Hal left in a rage. They embarked on an expensive custody battle over their two little boys and eventually were given a divorce. Then, after six months, Hal returned home. Now they are living together again, trying to work through a rather tumultuous relationship. "We can't wait to get into bed," Joan told us the last time we saw her. "My coworkers at the bank would never believe that it was me. I really let my hair down now." Joan and Hal are discussing remarriage at the present time.

Angela tried very hard to stay with Rick, her bisexual husband. He promised he would not have any more affairs with men but could not keep his promise. They were divorced after a long effort to maintain their marriage. Angela has since remarried and is pregnant. Rick has moved in with Geraldo.

Phil, who became so angry at his wife, Ellen, that he tried to throw her off a bridge, went through therapy and rebuilt his relationship with her. Phil still worries, because he cannot forget Ellen's affair and occasionally they still fight over it. Still, to all outward appearances, they are the ideal couple raising children, active in their church, and contributing to various civic organizations.

Marilyn seemed to fare the worst of anyone in the group. She still has not resolved her feelings of abandonment and cannot accept the fact that Carl, her doctor-husband, has married another woman. Marilyn has been looking for employment for the past two years and has tried an assortment of unskilled jobs, working at a cosmetic counter in a department store, as a receptionist for a finance company, and as a travel agent. "I can't make the adjustment," she says.

Craig and Sandy have stayed together. They adopted a "swinging" life-style and swap with their friends, Beth and Guy, on a regular basis. Craig still expresses some jealousy about his wife going to bed with Guy, but for the time being he accepts the arrangement. As he says, "It ain't perfect. Don't know how long it will last."

Francine had great difficulty in admitting that Alan was having an affair, and when she could no longer deny what was taking place she slipped into a deep depression. Eventually, after trying to commit suicide, she took a firm hold on her life, returned to school, and now holds a respectable job. She and Alan have been separated for three years but have not yet gone through a divorce. Francine dates other men and occasionally sees Alan.

Gerald never got over Marina's affair. After they separated he would follow her and check on who she was seeing. One evening they were both invited by a friend to the same party. Gerald was drinking and he told Marina she would have to return home with him. When she refused, he grabbed a knife from the kitchen drawer and attempted to stab her, but only cut her arm. He is presently out on bail.

Some of the group members have still not picked the last petal off the flower, have not said the last "love me, love me not." Maybe they never will. But the choice is there, for them, and for anyone who experiences betrayal.

Index

About the Authors

Therapists Daniel J. Dolesh and Sherelynn Lehman co-host the weekly call-in radio show *Sexline* in Cleveland, and as a team they speak and conduct workshops on sexuality and human relations throughout the country. Sherry Lehman appears weekly as the staff family and sex therapist for NBC-TV in Cleveland, and is a member of the Case Western Reserve University Gender Identity Clinic. Dan Dolesh is president of the Values and Human Sexuality Institute in Washington, D.C., and has chaired the National Parenting Committee and the National Committee for Human Sexuality Education. Both authors commute weekly between Cleveland and Washington, where they have private therapy practices.